Elite • 146

The Yugoslav Wars (2)

Bosnia, Kosovo and Macedonia 1992–2001

Dr N Thomas & K Mikulan • Illustrated by D Pavlovic

Consultant editor Martin Windrow

First published in Great Britain in 2006 by Osprey Publishing,
Midland House, West Way, Botley, Oxford OX2 0PH, UK
443 Park Avenue South, New York, NY 10016, USA
E-mail: info@ospreypublishing.com

ISBN 13: 978 1 84176 964 6

Editor: Martin Windrow
Page Layouts by Ken Vail Graphic Design, Cambridge, UK (www.kvgd.com)
Typeset in New Baskerville and Helvetica
Index by Glyn Sutcliffe
Originated by PPS Grasmere Ltd, Leeds, UK
Printed in China through World Print Ltd.

08 09 10 11 12 11 10 9 8 7 6 5 4 3 2

A CIP catalogue record for this book is available from the British Library

FOR A CATALOGUE OF ALL BOOKS PUBLISHED BY OSPREY MILITARY
AND AVIATION PLEASE CONTACT:

NORTH AMERICA
Osprey Direct
c/o Random House Distribution Centre, 400 Hahn Road, Westminster,
MD 21157 USA
Email: info@ospreydirect.com

ALL OTHER REGIONS
Osprey Direct UK, P.O. Box 140 Wellingborough, Northants, NN8 2FA, UK
E-mail: info@ospreydirect.co.uk

Buy online at www.ospreypublishing.com

Editor's Note

Due to the complexities of the conflicts described, a number
of armed forces – particularly the Yugoslav and Croatian
armies, and Serbian and Croatian militias – figure in both
volumes of this study. Readers will find it helpful to keep the
first volume – Elite 138, *The Yugoslav Wars (1) Slovenia &
Croatia, 1991–95* – to hand while reading this text.

Acknowledgements

Nigel Thomas would like to thank his wife Heather and their
sons Alexander and especially Dominick for their
encouragement and support. Krunoslav Mikulan would like
to thank Henrik Clausen, Davor Marijan, Sinisa Pogacic,
Borivoj Radojcic, Emil Smutni and Vladimir Trendafilovski;
and also his wife Rolanda and their son Bruno, to whom he
is deeply indebted for their help and support during the time
he spent resarching this work.

Artist's Note

Readers may care to note that the original paintings from
which the colour plates in this book were prepared are
available for private sale. All reproduction copyright
whatsoever is retained by the Publishers. All enquiries
should be addressed to:

Darko Pavlovic, Modecova 3, Zagreb, 10090, Croatia

The Publishers regret that they can enter into no
correspondence upon this matter.

GLOSSARY OF MILITARY & NATIONAL ACRONYMS

AKSH	Albanian National Army	NO	People's Defence Force, Autonomous Province of W Bosnia	SDG	Serbian Volunteer Guard
ABiH	Bosnian-Moslem Army			SDS	Serbian Democratic Party
ARK	Krajina Autonomous Region			SG	Serbian Guard
ARM	Macedonian Army	OS BiH	Armed Forces of Bosnia-Herzegovina	SHS	Kingdom of the Serbs, Croats and Slovenes (pre-1941)
BiH	Bosnia-Herzegovina				
FYROM	Former Yugoslav Republic of Macedonia	OUP	Department of Internal Affairs	SOS	Bosnian-Serb Army (April 1992)
		OSRBiH	Armed Forces of the Republic of Bosnia-Herzegovina	SVK	Serbian Army of Krajina
HDZBiH	Croatian Democratic Union of Bosnia-Herzgovina			TORBiH	Bosnian-Moslem Territorial Defence Force
		PJM/PJP	Serbian Special Police (before/from 1996)		
HOS	Croatian Defence Forces			UÇK	Kosova Liberation Army
HV	Croatian Army	PL	Patriotic League	UÇK/NMET	National Liberation Army (Black Mountains & Tetovo)
JNA	Yugoslav People's Army	RDB	Serbian State Security Department		
JSO	Special Operations Unit	RS	*Republika Srpska* (Republic of Srpska)	UÇPMB	Presevo, Medvedja & Bujanovac Liberation Army
KPS	Kosovo Police Service				
LDK	Democratic League of Kosova	RSK	Republic of Serbian Krajina	UDBa	Yugoslav Security Service
MD	Military District	RV i PO	Yugoslav Air Force	VF	Federation Armed Forces
MHVO	Moslem-Croat Defence Council	SAJ	Special Counter-terrorist Unit	VF-B	Bosnian-Moslem Component (of VF)
MUP	Bosnian, Herceg Bosna & Serb Min of Internal Affairs	SAO	Serbian Autonomous Region		
		SCP	Serbian Chetnik Movement	VF-H	Bosnian-Croat Component (of VF)
MVR	Macedonian Interior Ministry	SDA	(Moslem) Party of Democratic Action	VJ	Yugoslav Army
NDH	Independent State of Croatia (1941–45)			VRS	Bosnian-Serb Army (May 1992)
		SDB	State Security Service		

THE YUGOSLAV WARS (2) BOSNIA-HERZEGOVINA, KOSOVO & MACEDONIA 1992–2001

Two elderly Bosnian TO privates photographed before 1992, in distinctive grey-blue uniforms introduced in Bosnia in the 1980s and worn until replacement by JNA olive-grey or camouflage uniforms. Note the red cloth star on the front of the sidecap, and a Bosnian flag on the left side – a red patch, with the old flag of Communist Yugoslavia at top left. (Unless specifically credited otherwise, all photos reproduced in this book are from the authors' collection)

BOSNIA-HERZEGOVINA

On 2 December 1945, President Tito proclaimed the Federative People's Republic of Yugoslavia as a one-party state, with Bosnia-Herzegovina as one of six constituent republics.[1] Islam was officially discouraged, but from 1968 Bosnian-Moslems were regarded as an ethnic group.[2]

By mid-1990 three communal parties had succeeded the Communist Party in Bosnia. Alija Izetbegovic's Bosnian-Moslem ('Bosniac') SDA wanted to preserve Bosnia; the Bosnian-Croat HDZBiH aimed, after Feb 1992, for secession and annexation to Croatia; and Radovan Karadzic's Bosnian-Serb SDS planned secession and annexation to Serbia.

The SDA won Bosnia's first free elections in December 1990, and on 20 December Izetbegovic took power as president, heading an SDA-SDS-HDZBiH coalition government. However, in September 1991 Karadzic declared Bosnian-Serb autonomy, obtained Yugoslav People's Army (JNA) intervention to 'protect' the Bosnian-Serbs, and from mid-1991 began to smuggle in weapons from Serbia. Izetbegovic had no wish to remain in a Serbian-dominated rump Yugoslavia following the independence of Croatia, and called a national referendum which recommended independence. President Izetbegovic proclaimed the Republic of Bosnia-Herzegovina on 3 March 1992.

In spring 1991 Bosnia had a population of 4,354,911, of whom 44 per cent were Bosnian-Moslems,

---

1 For a brief introduction to the historical background of the South Slav lands pre-1945, see Elite 138, *The Yugoslav Wars (1): Slovenia & Croatia 1991–95*.
For the sake of brevity, Bosnia-Herzegovina will be referred to simply as 'Bosnia' hereafter in this text.

2 Note that throughout this text, distinct communities within a republic or province are described by this order of words, e.g. 'Bosnian-Moslems' meaning Moslems living in Bosnia.

31 per cent Bosnian-Serbs, 17 per cent Bosnian-Croats, and 8 per cent other minorities. Of Bosnia's 109 districts, 28 had a majority of Bosnian-Moslems, 31 of Bosnian-Serbs, 14 of Bosnian-Croats, and 36 districts had no majority. Formerly Bosnia spoke Serbo-Croat, but now split into separate entities speaking three languages: Serbian (Cyrillic alphabet), Croatian, and Bosnian (Latin alphabet).

The Serbian Autonomous Regions (SAOs) were established from September 1991, and on 9 January 1992 united into the Serbian Republic of Bosnia-Herzegovina, later Republic of Srpska *(Republika Srpska)*. The Bosnian-Croats established two regions in western Herzegovina and Posavina in November 1991, and by April 1992 united them in the Community of Herceg Bosna (28 August 1993, 'Republic'). The Bosnian-Moslem Republic of Bosnia-Herzegovina under Izetbegovic was therefore restricted to central Bosnia (with four Bosnian-Croat enclaves) and the Sarajevo, Srebrenica, Zepa and Gorazde enclaves.

BOSNIAN PRESIDENCY
Territorial Defence Force

In 1988 the Yugoslav Army had placed the Bosnian provincial Territorial Defence Force under 1 Military District (Belgrade), and reduced its strength by two-thirds to 86,362 in Dec 1991. This Bosnian *Teritorijalna odbrana* (TO), commanded by Bosnian-Serb generals, comprised nine regions. Each region *(okrug)* controlled about 12 districts (totalling 109), with a light artillery battery, a pontoon engineer company, sometimes an AA battalion, and two to six 1,800-strong TO brigades (26 in total); each brigade had four company- or battalion-sized detachments *(odred)*.

Bosnian-Moslem capacity to defend themselves was weakened by Izetbegovic's vain attempts to retain good relations with the JNA, and he naively gave control of the TO to the Bosnian-Serb SDS in the coalition government. On 19 Dec 1990 the SDA, alarmed by the SDS's secessionist attitudes, discussed forming a military organization; and in Mar 1991 Sefer Halilovic formed the Patriotic League *(Patriotska liga –* PL) as an independent Bosnian army, with the same territorial organization as the TO. The PL received training at Croatian Special Police centres, and by Mar 1992 claimed 98,000 trained troops – more than the shrinking TO – organized in 9 regions and 103 (out of 109) districts.

On 1 Nov 1991 the JNA, Bosnian-Serb and Serbian paramilitary militias began attacking Bosnian-Moslem and Bosnian-Croat towns and villages including Sarajevo, and on 3 Mar 1992 fighting started in Bosanski Brod. On 4 Apr Izetbegovic ordered general mobilization; and on 8 Apr he transformed the Sarajevo TO command into the GHQ of the *Teritorijalna odbrana Republike Bosne i Hercegovine* (TORBiH), appointing the Bosnian-Moslem Col Hasan Efendic as commander. Colonel Stjepan Siber, a Bosnian-Croat, became chief-of-staff, and Col Jovan Divjak, a Bosnian-Serb, his deputy. Seven out of nine TO Regional HQs joined the TORBiH (Banja Luka and Doboj refused), bringing in 73 districts with Moslem and Bosnian-Croat majorities; 36 with Bosnian-Serb majorities refused. The TORBiH was formally established on 15 Apr, when all Patriotic League units joined the force.

Brigadni general **Atif Dudakovic, ABiH 5 Corps commander, 1994, wearing a green beret, and the first pattern breast rank badge without gold edging (see chart on page 56, item 5). The beret badge is the same coat-of-arms on crossed swords as in the rank insignia, in a gold wreath. General Dudakovic's successful defence of the Bihac Pocket in north-west Bosnia from April 1992 to October 1995 was an impressive achievement; he later commanded the Bosnian Federation Armed Forces.**

**BOSNIAN, KOSOVO & MACEDONIAN
CONFLICTS
1 November 1991 - 13 August 2001**

In April 1992 the TORBiH's 75,000 strength included about 7,500 Bosnian-Serbs and 7,500 Bosnian-Croats, while about 30 per cent of the officers were Bosnian-Serbs or Bosnian-Croats. The Bosnian Presidency forces were reorganized into four regions (Bihac, Sarajevo, Tuzla and Zenica) and two tactical groups (TGs) controlling TO, PL and newly formed units. There were soon 26 brigades (named after districts), plus a Special Forces unit, a number of independent battalions and detachments, and military police, armoured and mixed artillery battalions – a hastily organized and woefully under-armed force. A brigade *(brigada)* had an establishment of 1,500 but often only a true strength of about 500, short of all kinds of weapons and with minimal artillery, armour, signals or engineer equipment. The 1st and 2nd TGs were formed in unsuccessful attempts to lift the siege of Sarajevo.

On 20 May 1992 the TORBiH, PL, other militias and the Bosnian-Croat HVO and HOS were officially united as the Armed Forces of the Republic of Bosnia-Herzegovina (*Oruzane snage Republike Bosne i Hercegovine* – OSRBiH). On 23 May Col Efendic was replaced as commander by Sefer Halilovic.

Bosnian Army

On 20 May 1992 the TORBiH was renamed *Armija Republike Bosne i Hercegovine* – ARBiH, usually abbreviated ABiH); and in Nov 1993, Halilovic was replaced in command by Rasim Delic. The ABiH, now 80,000 strong, was reorganized on 18 Aug 1992 into a more conventional structure. Initially four corps were established: 1 Corps (Sarajevo); 2 (Tuzla), in northern Bosnia; 3 (Zenica) & 4 (Mostar), in Herzegovina; plus the East Bosnian Operational Group in the vulnerable eastern enclave of Gorazde. 5 (Bihac) Corps was established on 21 Oct 1992 from the Una-Sana OPG (*Operativna grupa* – Operational Group), to defend the NW Bosnian enclave; while 7 (Travnik) Corps was formed on 7 Apr 1994 with brigades from 3 Corps, to advance north-westwards through southern Bosnia. 6 (Konjic) Corps was formed in June 1993 from 4 Corps' Northern Herzegovina OPG, to occupy northern Herzegovina from the HVO and eventually reach the Adriatic coast; it had little success, however, and was disbanded on 27 Feb 1994.

Each corps *(Korpus)* controlled a number of brigades, independent battalions and companies. Brigades were designated as infantry, mountain, motorized or light, and given new three-digit numbers, the first indicating the corps. The larger 1–3 Corps comprised 15 OPGs, each with 3–7 brigades. From Aug 1992 to Dec 1994 about 105 ABiH brigades were formed or re-formed in the 1-527 series: 48 infantry or undesignated, 41 mountain, 10 motorized and 6 light – but not all existed at the same time. There were also single commando and reconnaissance, MP and artillery brigades; and various independent units included the Delta SF Unit, four commando detachments, six

Men of 5 Coy, 2 Bn, 502 Mountain Bde of 5 Corps, ABiH, holding a trench in the Bihac Pocket, 1993. They are poorly equipped, wearing a mixture of different camouflage and civilian clothing items typical of the Bosnian Army before 1995; but the confidence and determination in their faces is evident.

Corps HQ MP battalions, a mixed artillery battalion and an independent armoured company. Eight Bosnian-Croat HVO units were permanently incorporated into the ABiH. The 'Black Swans' *(Crni labudovi)* Islamic PL unit, formed in Apr 1992 in Konjic under 4 Corps (later 1 Corps), eventually numbered 800 men; it earned a reputation for battlefield bravery, but also for attacks on Bosnian-Serb and Bosnian-Croat civilians.

Table 1: Battle Order of Bosnia-Herzegovina Territorial Defence Force, May–Aug 1992

GHQ, Sarajevo (Sefer Halilovic)

Special Units

Regional TO HQ Sarajevo

1 Sanjak Bde, 1 Dobrinja Bde, 1 Stup Bde, 1 Drina Valley Bde, 1 Ilidza Bde, 11 Inf Bde 'Dragon of Bosnia', 12 Inf Bde 'Hadzi Lojo', 13 New Sarajevo Bde; 14 Pofalic-Velesic Inf Bde, 15 Novi Grad Inf Bde, 'Isa Beg Isakovic' Bde, Sarajevo District MP Bn, ind dets & bns

Regional TO HQ Tuzla – N Bosnia

1–3 Tuzla Bdes, 1 Lukavac Bde, ind dets & bns

Regional TO HQ Zenica – Central Bosnia

1 & 2 Zenica Bdes, 1 & 7 Bosnian Krajina Bdes, ind dets & bns

Regional TO HQ Bihac /Una-Sana Operational Group – NW Bosnia

1 & 2 Bihac Bdes; 1 Cazin Bde, 101 Bde (Velika Kladusa), 105 Bde (Buzim), 111 Bde (Bosanska Krupa), Special Duties Det (Bihac), 1 Bihac Armd Bn, 14 ind dets

1 Tactical Group (Konjic) – W Herzegovina

111 Bde (Konjic)

2 Tactical Group (Hadzici-Trnovo) – Sarajevo

'Nijaz Kulenović' Rgt, 'Igman' Combined Det & 'Igman' Mix Arty Bn (Hadzici)

Abbreviations for this and all other Tables: AA = Anti-aircraft, AF = Air Force, Armd = Armoured, AT = Anti-tank, Arty = Artillery, Bn = Battalion, Cdo = Commando, Coy = Company, Det = Detachment, Div = Division, Eng = Engineer, Gds = Guards, HDB = Home Defence Bn, Hcptr = Helicopter, HDR = Home Defence Rgt, Ind = Independent, Inf = Infantry, Lt =

Light, Log = Logistics, MP = Military Police, Mech = Mechanized, Miss = Missile, Mix = Mixed, Mos = Moslem, Mot = Motorized, MT = Motor Transport, Mtn = Mountain, OPG = Operational Group, OZ = Operational Zone, Pont = Pontoon, Prot = Protection, Recon = Reconnaissance, Rgt = Regiment, Sig = Signal, Sqdn = Squadron, TG = Tactical Group

Between 17 Aug 1992 and 23 Feb 1994, relations between the HVO and local ABiH forces varied widely: the Croats co-operated with ABiH 1, 2 & 5 Corps, but there were constant territorial disputes with 3, 4 & 6 Corps, leading to a destructive 'war within a war'. The US-brokered Washington Agreement of 18 Mar 1994 finally regularized relations, establishing the Federation of Bosnia-Herzegovina and creating a permanent Moslem-Croat alliance which prevented a Bosnian-Serb military victory. By June 1994 the ABiH was the numerically strongest armed force, with 110,000 men and 100,000 reserves, against 80,000 in the Bosnian-Serb VRS and 50,000 in the Bosnian-Croat HVO.

In Jan 1995 the ABiH, now expanded to 150,000–200,000, was reorganized. The OPGs in 1, 2, 3 & 7 Corps were redesignated as divisions, each *divizija* comprising 3–6 brigades; however, 4 and 5 Corps retained their brigades. It was a much improved fighting force, but the UN arms embargo left it critically short of equipment, with only 40 tanks, 30 APCs, and small arms for only 50,000 men. The ABiH gained victories in operations in 1995, but was heavily reliant on HVO units. Bosnian-Moslem efforts helped achieve the Dayton Agreement of 14 Dec 1995, but never the clear military victories their sacrifices deserved. After Dayton the ABiH and HVO merged as the Bosnian Federal Army *(Vojska Federacije Bosne i Hercegovine)*.

Table 2: Battle Order of Bosnia-Herzegovina Army, Aug 1992–Dec 1994

GHQ, Sarajevo

(Sefer Halilovic, later *Armijski general* Rasim Delic)
MP Guard Bn (later Bde), Special Unit 'Delta'

1 Corps, Sarajevo

(Mustafa Hajrulahovic, *Brigadni general* Vahid Karavelic & *Brigadir* Nedzad Ajnadzic)
1 OPG (Bjelasnica, Igman, Treskavica Mtns)
2 OPG (Visoko)
3 OPG (Nisic Range and Cemerska Mtns)
1 Mtn Bde; 2 Mot Bde (Novi Grad); 2 Mtn Bde (Stari Grad); 3 Bde; 4 Mot Bde (Ilidza); 5 Mot Bde (Novi Grad); 6 Mot Bde; 8 Mtn Bde; 9 Mtn Bde (Hadzici); 10 Mtn Bde; 15 Mot Bde; 82 Foca Bde; 1 Bosniak Bde; Croatian Bde 'King Tvrtko' (part of HVO until Oct 1993); MP Bn

2 Corps, Tuzla

(*Pukovnik* Zeljko Knez, *Brigadni general* Hazim Sadic & *Brigadir* Sead Delic)
1 OPG, later 21 Div (Gradacac): 107 Mot Bde (Gradacac) – ex HVO; 108 Mot Bde (Breko) – ex HVO
2 OPG, later 22 Div (Gracanica): 109 Mtn Bde (Doboj) – ex HVO; 111 Bde (Gracanica); 117 Bde (Lukavac)
3 OPG, later 23 Div (Kladanj): 1 Olovo Bde; 121 Mtn Bde (Kladanj)
4 OPG, later 24 Div (Kalesija): 206 Mtn Bde (Zvornik); 207 Mtn Bde (Tesanj)
5 OPG, later 25 Div (Tuzla): 1–3 Tuzla Bdes
6 OPG, later 26 Div (Zivinice): 119 Mtn Bde (Banovici)
7/ South OPG (Tesanj): 201 Bde (Maglaj); 202 Mtn Bde (Teslic), based Tesanj; 203 Mot Bde (Doboj); 204 Mtn Bde (Teslic); (Nov 1994, OPG to 3 Corps)
8 OPG, later 28 Div (Srebrenica): 1 'Berbir' Bde (Bosanska Gradiska); 1 Mos Drina Valley Bde (Kladanj); 101 Bde (Zepa); 114 E Bosnian Bde (Srebrenica); Potocari & Suceska Bdes, '3 May' Bde (Kraljivode); Cdo Det 'Wasps' (Zivinice); Cdo Det 'Silj Knights' (Doboj); Cdo Det 'Black Wolves' (Kalesija); Ind Bn (Sokolac); MP Bn (Tuzla)
HVO units acting in coordination with 2 Corps: 108 Bde (Brcko), 110 Bde (Usora) & 115 Bde 'Zrinski' (Drijenca-Tuzla)

3 Corps, Zenica

(Enver Hadzihasanovic, *Brigadir* Mehmed Alagic & *Brigadir* Sahib Mahmuljin)
Bosnian Krajina OPG (Travnik): 27 Mtn Bde; 306 & 312 Bdes (Travnik)
Bosnia OPG (Zavidovici): 303 Mtn Bde (Zenica); 318 Mtn Bde (Zavidovici); 319 Mtn Bde (Zepce)
West OPG (Bugojno): 307 Mot Bde (Bugojno); 308 Mtn Bde (Novi Travnik); 317 Bde (Gornji Vakuf)
Lasva OPG (Kakanj): 305 Bde (Jajce-Biljesevo); 325 Mtn Bde (Vitez); 333 Bde (Busovaca)
7/ South OPG (until Nov 1994 in 2nd Corps; 1995, 37 Div): 7 Mos Mtn *(Mujahedin)*, 301 Mot & 314 Mtn Bdes & MP Bn (Zenica); 17 Krajina Mtn Bde (Travnik); 37 Mos Lt Bde; 299 Lt Bde; 302 (later 315) Bde (Visoko); 304 Mtn Bde (Breza); 309 & 329 Mtn & 311 (ex-309 & 311) Lt Bdes (Kakanj); 310 Mtn Bde (Breza-Fojnica); 316 Bde (Fojnica); 320 Mtn Bde; 322 Mtn Bde (Vares); 323 Bde (Kiseljak); 330 Lt Bde; 370 Mtn Bde (Donji Vakuf – Bugojno); Cdo & Recon Bde; 'El Mujaheed' Unit (foreign volunteers)

4 Corps, Mostar

(*Pukovnik* Arif Pasalic, Sulejman Budakovic, *Brigadni general* Ramiz Drekovic & *Brigadir* Mustafa Polutak)
41 Mot (ex-1 Mostar), 42 & 49 Mtn Bdes & MP Bn (Mostar); 43 Mtn Bde (Konjic); 44 Mtn Bde (Jablanica); 45 Mtn Bde 'Neretvica' (Buturovic Polje, near Jablanica); 48 Mtn Bde (Mostar); 4 Mos Lt Bde; 19 E Herzegovina Lt Bde; Ind Bn (Prozor); ind dets

5 Corps, Bihac

(Ramiz Drekovic, Mustafa Hajrulahoviz & *Brigadir/Brigadni general/Divizijski general* Atif Dudakovič)
501 & 502 Mtn Bdes, MP & 101 HVO Bns (Bihac); 503 & 517 Bdes (Cazin); 504 Bde; 505 Mot Bde 'Gazije' (Buzim); 506 Bde; 511 Bde (Bosanska Krupa); 521 & 527 Mtn Bdes (Velika Kladusa); Cdo Det 'Sana Flies'; Mix Arty Bn

6 Corps, Konjic

43 Mtn Bde (Konjic); 44 & 45 'Neretvica' Mtn Bdes (Jablanica)

7 Corps, Travnik

(Mehmed Alagić)
17 Krajina, 306 Mtn & 312 Bdes & MP Bn (Travnik); 27 Mtn Bde; 37 Mos Lt Bde; 305 Bde (Jajce); 307 Mot Bde (Bugojno); 308 Bde (Novi Travnik); 317 Bde (Gornji Vakuf); 325 Bde (Vitez); 333 Bde (Busovaca); 370 Bde (Donji Vakuf); Indep Armd Coy

E Bosnian OPG, Gorazde (later 81 Div):
1 Rogatica Bde; 1 Visegrad Bde; 1 Gorazde Bde

Foreign volunteers

From June 1992, about 3,000 Moslem *Mujahedin* ('holy warriors') from Afghanistan, Albania, Chechnya, Egypt, Iran, Jordan, Lebanon, Pakistan, Saudi Arabia, Sudan, Turkey and Yemen served in the ABiH. 7 Moslem Mountain Bde (3 Corps) was formed in Oct 1992, and by Dec 1995 six more Moslem light brigades – 4, 9, 17, 447, 448 and 807 – all seven being redesignated Moslem Liberation Brigades. Each 2,000-strong *Muslimanska oslobodilacka brigada*, including about 750–1,000 *Mujahedin*, was allocated to a different corps. The el-Mudzahedin Detachment was formed in Travnik on 13 Aug 1993 with 600 Bosnian-Moslems and 200 *Mujahedin*, serving from 6 Sept under Bosanska Krajina OPG. All foreign volunteers were required to leave Bosnia under the Dayton Agreement, but some stayed, having acquired Bosnian citizenship through marriage. There is no evidence that al-Qa'ida influence was especially strong in Bosnia.

An officer of a Bosnian Special Police Unit, 1991. Just before the outbreak of war the Special Police purchased a quantity of US Army camouflage uniforms – as here, worn under a sleeveless load-carrying vest. Most Special Police still wore one of the three tiger-stripe camouflage patterns, but others were later introduced. Most Special Police, like this officer, wore the pre-1992 Police red cap star as their only insignia, senior officers adding shoulder straps with rank badges.

Other Bosnian-Moslem forces

After the absorption by the TORBiH in Apr 1992, some PL units – including 3 PL Bde (Zenica) – still operated independently, and the PL supported the ABiH 3 Corps attack on HVO-held Zenica in Apr 1993. PL personnel wore green berets, as did many ABiH units, but there was no separate 'Green Berets' organization.

The ABiH assigned 15 mixed aircraft to corps HQs, to supply 5 Corps in Bihac and 2 Corps units in the Gorazde, Srebrenica and Zepa enclaves. There were no naval forces.

The Yugoslav Constitution of 21 Feb 1974 had decentralized the police, and thereafter the Bosnian Police reported to the Bosnian Interior Ministry (*Ministarstvo unutrasnjih poslova* – MUP) in Sarajevo. The Bosnian Police *(Policija Republike Bosne i Hercegovine)* were formed in April 1992 from districts under Bosnian-Moslem control, and there was also a Special Police Unit *(Specijalna jedinica)*.

REPUBLIKA SRPSKA

The Bosnian-Serbs in 51 districts (including 11 with Moslem majorities) formed six Serbian Autonomous Regions (SAOs):

Autonomous Region of Krajina (ARK), capital Banja Luka, formed in Apr 1991 with 15 districts in W Bosnia. It was the largest region, but after failure to merge with *SAO Krajina* in Croatia it was renamed Bosnian Krajina *(SAO Bosanska Krajina)* in Sept 1991.

NE Bosnia *(SAO Sjevernoistocna Bosna)*, capital Bijeljina, formed Sept 1991 with five districts; renamed *SAO Semberija* in Nov 1991, and *SAO Semberija i Majevica* in Dec 1991.

N Bosnia *(SAO Ozren-Posavina)*, capital Doboj, formed Nov 1991, with Doboj District, intended to link Bosnian Krajina with Semberija & Majevica, but never fully established.

Ozren-Posavina *(SAO Sjeverna Bosna)*, planned from predominantly Moslem and Croat districts in northern Bosnia, but not fully established.

Romanija *(SAO Romanija)*, formed Sept 1991, and *SAO Birac*, formed Nov 1991, combined in Nov 1991 as *SAO Romanija-Birac*, with 15 districts, capital Pale.

A soldier of the Bosnian 5 Corps; equipment is limited to a belt and an M70 assault rifle. Although his faded, four-colour leaf-pattern camouflage uniform shows no insignia, the *5.Korpus* badge was a white winged horse rearing to the left, on a black or very dark green shield edged white.

Herzegovina *(SAO Hercegovina)*, capital Bileca, formed Sept 1991, with seven districts in E Herzegorina.

In Mar 1992, Radovan Karadzic unified the SAOs as the Serb Republic of Bosnia-Herzegovina, renamed 12 Aug simply as the Serb Republic (*Republika Srpska* – RS) with himself as president. Karadzic envisaged a Serbian state joined to Croatian Krajina and Serbia proper, with access to the Adriatic in southern Dalmatia. The official capital comprised the three Bosnian-Serb controlled districts of Sarajevo (Ilidza, New Sarajevo and Vogosca), but Banja Luka was the de facto capital.

Republika Srpska Army

When hostilities broke out on 3 Mar 1992 the eight corps-sized JNA units in Bosnia supported the Bosnian-Serbs. On 8 May the JNA was redesignated the Army of Yugoslavia (*Vojska Jugoslavije* – VJ), and

The notorious Bosnian-Serb military commander, Ratko Mladic, in 1994. He wears the VRS M92 version of the distinctive M08 Serbian officers' peaked service cap, which the VRS also produced in tiger-stripe camouflage. Note the cap cord and badge for general officers, the latter with the red-blue-white Serbian colours in the central cartouche; the cap braids of a *general-potpukovnik* (two-star general); and his left breast rank patch, a gilt metal wreathed sword-&-baton above two bars. Sought for trial by the International Criminal Tribunal for former Yugoslavia (ICTY), at the time of writing (June 2006) Mladic is still at large.

immediately evacuated about 14,000 troops from Bosnia, leaving about 80,000 to form the Bosnian-Serb Army. After several interim titles, on 12 Aug 1992 the former HQ of the JNA's Banja Luka Corps was finally renamed the Army of the Serb Republic (*Vojska Republike Srpske* – VRS), under Gen Ratko Mladic, the Bosnian-Serb commander of the VJ's 2 Military District.

The VRS maintained JNA organization, equipment, uniforms and traditions. The GHQ was at Pale, 20 miles east of Sarajevo; and the eight JNA formations were re-formed into six VRS corps stationed in the SAOs comprising *Republika Srpska*:

1 Krajina Corps (HQ Banja Luka), ex-Banja Luka Corps, in northern Bosnian Krajina and Ozren-Pozavina.

2 Krajina Corps (HQ Drvar), ex-Bihac Corps, in southern Bosnian Krajina.

3 East Bosnian Corps (HQ Bijeljina), ex-Tuzla Corps, in Semberija & Majevica.

4 Sarajevo-Romanija Corps (HQ Pale), ex-Sarajevo Corps, in Romanija-Birac.

5 Drina Corps, formed with 4 & 6 Corps units in southern Romanija-Birac and northern Herzegovina.

6 Herzegovina Corps (HQ Bileca), ex-Trebinje-Bileca OPG, in eastern Herzegovina.

The VRS comprised redesignated JNA, TO and newly raised VRS units. There were 77 'brigades' (often 500-strong battalions): 2 armoured, 7 motorized, 22 infantry or undesignated, and 46 light infantry. Most

The Orthodox Church played a key role in defining Serbian nationalism. Here three VRS general officers participate in a military ceremony with a priest, 1995.

corps contained 5–13 brigades, but 1 Krajina Corps, with 33, was effectively a double corps, containing both armoured brigades, almost half the motorized and more than half the light infantry brigades. These troops were organized into 10 and 30 Divs; 1–5 TGs; Doboj, Prijedor & Vlasic OPGs; and the Group of Light Brigades. The VRS was primarily an infantry force, with its inadequate support units and services allocated to corps HQs and 1 Krajina Corps taking the lion's share.

Foreign volunteers

Up to 4,000 foreign Orthodox Christians may have joined the VRS or Serbian militias. A hundred-strong Greek Volunteer Guard was formed in Mar 1995, and fought with 5 Drina Corps at Srebrenica in July 2005. Romanian volunteers fought near Sarajevo in 1992, and Ukrainians were also reported. About 700 Russians fought for the VRS, and at least four Russian units were formed; the most effective was the Tsarist Wolves commanded by Alexander Mukharev, including a Cossack company under Alexander Zagrebov, famous for the defence of Zaglavak Hill in winter 1993. Valery Vlasenko formed a unit near Visegrad in Sept 1992; another was led by Lt Alexander Alexandrov (kia May 1993 near Visegrad); and one under Alexander Shkrabov (kia June 1994) fought in Sarajevo in 1993–4.

Other Bosnian-Serb forces

The VRS Air Force & AA Artillery was established in May 1992 under MajGen Zivomir Ninkovic, with 4 squadrons formed from JNA units from Slovenia and Croatia: 74 (ex-JNA 474) Air Base at Mahovljani, near Banja Luka, comprised 27 (ex-237) and 28 (ex-238) Fighter-Bomber Sqns from JNA 82 Aviation Bde in Slovenia. The helicopter units at Zaluzani AB near Banja Luka had originally formed part of 111 Av Bde at Zagreb-Pleso in Croatia, and comprised 11 Hcptr Rgt with 711 AT Sqn and 780 Tspt Squadron. On 26 July 1992, 11 Hcptr Rgt disbanded and 92 Mixed Air Bde formed with its 4 squadrons; later in 1992, 711 & 780 Sqns merged as 89 Mixed Hcptr Squadron. Meanwhile 92 Lt Mixed Sqn was formed with three flights at Bratunac, Prijedor and Zaluzani. The AA force comprised 155 Miss Bde and a missile regiment.

The Air Force conducted 17,316 combat sorties and medical evacuations during the Bosnian War, losing 11 aircraft and 7 helicopters. No VRS naval forces were established.

The Police (*Milicija*, or from 1994 *Policija Republike Srpske*) operated in 51 districts, and included Special Police units and an air unit.

Serb militias

Over 20,000 Serbs and Bosnian-Serbs served in militias and paramilitary units, whose record surpassed the savagery they had displayed in Croatia in 1991. They were very active in E Bosnia in 1992–93, usually conducting mopping-up operations behind JNA units and against non-Serb villages, but several combined to attack and occupy the town of Zvornik 8–13 Apr 1992.

The White Eagles, Dusan the Mighty, SCP and SDG militias were financed and organized by the Yugoslav Security Service (*Sluzba drzavne*

A thoughtful young VRS conscript in 1992. On his tiger-stripe camouflage beret he displays the short-lived M91 Yugoslav Army metal cap badge (introduced October 1991): the JNA monogram centred on a disc striped blue-white-red, on crossed swords and rays. Next to it he has sewn (unofficially) the cloth patch of an élite unit – apparently a red oval edged gold, with gold laurel branches below a central motif in white on a dark colour.

Grim-faced VRS conscripts taking an oath of allegiance in 1995. The officer (bottom right) is wearing the M92 peaked service cap, with thin gold crown-piping and no chin strap, worn by field and company officers. The conscripts have peakless camouflage caps of the traditional Serb shape.

bezbednosti – SDB). They were supervised in the field by the SDB's 'Red Berets' *(Crvene Beretke)* unit, formed in 1991 and reporting to Franko 'Frenki' Simatovic. In 1992 the White Eagles *(Beli orlovi)* operated in Sarajevo, Gacko and Doboj, Zvornik and Bileca and Visegrad, Modrica, Bosanska Krupa, Banja Luka and Prijedor Districts. The Dusan the Mighty *(Dusan Silni)* militia fought at Zvornik in April 1992.

The Serbian Chetnik Movement *(Srpski cetnicki pokret* – SCP), under Vojislav Seselj, were active in Nevesinje, Kupres, Derventa, Modrica and Tuzla districts in 1992, and Kalinovik and Maglaj districts in 1993. The Serbian Volunteer Guard *(Srpska dobrovoljacka garda* – SDG), nicknamed 'Tigers' *(Tigrovi)* and led by Zeljko 'Arkan' Raznjatovic, operated in Teslic District in Mar

Table 3: Battle Order of Army of the Serb Republic of Bosnia-Herzegovina (SOS), 12 May–12 Aug 1992 & Republika Srpska Army (VRS) 12 Aug 1992–Oct 1995

GHQ, Pale

(General-potpukovnik/ General-pukovnik Ratko Mladic)
65th Prot Rgt; 10th Cdo Det

1 Krajina Corps (Banja Luka)

(General-major Momir Talic)
10 Div (disbanded late 1992); 30 Div (Srbobran, near Donji Vakuf); Temporary OPGs, 1–5 TGs; Doboj, Prijedor & Vlasic OPGs; Group of Lt Bdes (Banja Luka Tempo)
1 & 2 Armd Bdes; 16 Krajina Mot Bde (Banja Luka); 27 Mot Bde (Teslic); 43 Mot Bde; 11 Inf Bde (Bosanska Dubica); 19 Inf Bde (Srbobran, near Donji Vakuf); 5 Kozara Lt Inf Bde; 6 Lt Inf Bde (Sanski Most); 11 Lt Inf Bde (Mrkonjic-Grad); 12 Lt Inf Bde (Sipovo); 1 Novi Grad Lt Inf Bde (Bosanski Novi); 1–4 Banja Luka Lt Inf Bdes; 1 Celinac, 1 Doboj, 1 Gradiska, 1 Knezevo, 1 Kotor Varos, 1 & 2 Krajina, 1 Krnjina, 1 Laktasi, 1 Osinje, 1 & 2 Ozren, 1 Prnjavor, 1 Srbac, 1 Teslic, 1 Trebiska & 1 Vucjak Lt Inf Bdes; 1 Mix AT Bde; 1 & 9 Mix Arty Rgts; 1 Lt AA Rgt; 89 Miss Bde; 1 & 9 Eng Rgts; 1 Pont Bn; 1 & 9 Sig Bns; 1 MT Bn; 1 & 9 MP Bns

2 Krajina Corps (Drvar)

(General-major Grujo Boric)
7 Mot Bde (Kupres); 1 Lt Inf Bde & MP Bn (Drvar); 3 Lt Inf Bde (Srpski/ Bosanski Petrovac); 9 Lt Inf Bde (Grahovo); 11 Lt Inf Bde (Bosanska Krupa); 15 Lt Inf Bde (near Bihac); 17 Lt Inf Bde (Kljuc); 18 Lt Inf Bde; Glamoc Lt Inf Bde; three Mix Arty Bns

3 East Bosnian Corps (Bijeljina)

(General-major Novica Simic)
1–3 Posavina, 1–3 Semberija & 1–3 Majevica Bdes; 1 Zvornik Bde (later to Drina Corps); three Mix Arty Bns; MP Bn (Drvar)

4 Sarajevo-Romanija Corps (Pale)

(General-potpukovnik Stanislav Gavric, *General-major* Dragan Milosevic)
1 Sarajevo Mot Bde (Sarajevo-Lukavica); 2 Romanija Mot Bde (Knezina-Sokolac); 1 Romanija Inf Bde (Han Pijesak); Igman Inf Bde (Blazuj); Ilidza Inf Bde (Ilidza); Novo Sarajevo Inf Bde (Grbavica); 2 Sarajevo Lt Inf Bde (Vojkovici); Ilijas Inf Bde (Ilijas); Kosevo Lt Inf Bde (Radava); Rajlovac Lt Inf Bde (Rajlovac); Rogatica Lt Inf Bde (Rogatica); Trnovo Lt Inf Bde (Trnovo); Vogosca Lt Inf Bde (Vogosca); 4 Mix Arty Rgt (Pale); 4 Mix AT Rgt (Mokro-Pale); 4 Lt AA Rgt & 4 MP & 4 Sig Bns (Sarajevo-Lukavica); 4 Eng Bn (Pale)

5 Drina Corps

(General-major Milenko Zivanovic, *General-major* Radislav Krstic)
2 Romanija Mot Bde (Sokolac); 1 Zvornik Inf Bde (from 3 Corps); 1 Birac, 1 Bratunac, 1 & 5 Drina Valley, 1 Milici & 1 Vlasenica Lt Inf Bdes; Skelani Ind Inf Bn; 5 Mix Arty Rgt; 5 MP Bn; 5 Eng Bn; 5 Sig Bn

6 Herzegovina Corps (Bileca)

(General-major Radovan Grubac)
8 Mot Bde (Nevesinje); Mix Bde (Bileca); Bileca, Gacko & Trebinje Bdes; Gorazde Bde (near Gorazde); two Mix Arty Bns

1992, and assaulted Bijeljina town 1–4 Apr 1992, while its offshoot, the Serbian Armed Forces (*Srpske oruzane snage* – SOS), operated independently; the SDG was disbanded in Apr 1996. The SCP and SDG frequently operated jointly in 1992 in Sarajevo, Bosanski Samac, Visegrad, Banja Luka, Foca, Mostar and Brcko districts and the towns of Prijedor, Rogatica and Bratunac, as well as Odzak District in 1993.

A 110-strong detachment from 'Captain Dragan' Vasiljkovic's Krajina Serb Special Police unit fought at Zvornik Apr–May 1992, and later in Brcko and Zavidovici districts. In 1992 the *Garavi Sokak* operated in Gorazde district, the Grey Wolves *(Sivi vukovi)* in Bosanski Samac district, the Montenegro Guard *(Crnogorska garda)* in Foca district, and the Serbian Royalist Party's 600-strong Serbian Falcons *(Srpski jastrebovi)* and the Vukovar Unit *(Vukovarci)* in Zvornik and Foca. The Serbian Guard (*Srpska garda* – SG) from Serbia proper also fought in Bosnia.

An anxious or fatigued *Republika Srpska* policeman in 1995, wearing a mixture of insignia. On his blue beret is the M92 badge; but on the left sleeve of his blue-grey camouflage uniform is the ornate M95 patch, showing the Serbian coat-of-arms on a crowned, double-headed eagle.

HERCEG BOSNA
Croatian Defence Council

The political stance of the geographically fragmented Roman Catholic Bosnian-Croat community was ambivalent. Moderates wanted to remain in a united Bosnian state; nationalists wanted the Bosnian-Croatian dominated W Herzegovina and enclaves in Posavina and central Bosnia to be annexed to Croatia; and extreme nationalists wanted Croatia to annex all of Bosnia-Herzegovina, recreating the NDH of World War II. The HDZBiH party served in the coalition government in Dec 1990 under the moderate Stjepan Kljuic, who favoured a united Bosnia. However, following the JNA's destruction of Ravno village on 1 Nov 1991

General-pukovnik Ante Roso, the most successful HVO commander, in post from 12 November 1993 to 26 April 1994; like many participants in the Yugoslav Wars, Roso had previously served in the French Foreign Legion. That may be why he wears his dark green Special Forces beret pulled to the left in French fashion; the distinctive badge features the chequered red and white Croatian shield set on a triple oakleaf spray.

The commander of the Posusje District Special Unit, a locally raised armed force which was to be the Bosnian-Croats' first line of defence against the JNA in 1991. This unit's personnel wore Territorial Defence Force M70 greenish-brown berets, and obsolete JNA camouflage uniforms – here, in a horizontal tiger-stripe pattern of sand, leaf-green and chocolate-brown (see Plate A2).

without any intervention from the Bosnian-Moslems, the Bosnian-Croats determined to defend themselves. On 12 Nov 1991 the nationalist Mate Boban, supported by Croatian President Franjo Tudjman, established the Croat Community of Bosnian Posavina in N Bosnia; on 18 Nov he ousted Kljuic as HDZBiH leader and formed the Croat Community of Herceg Bosna (capital Mostar), in W Herzegovina and the central Bosnian enclaves of Kresevo, Travnik, Vares and Zepce. On 28 Aug 1993, Boban declared the Republic of Herceg Bosna with 30 districts.

The Bosnian-Croat army was formed in Apr 1992 as the Croatian Defence Council (*Hrvatsko vijece obrane* – HVO). It was commanded successively by Brig Milivoj Petkovic, MajGen Slobodan Praljak, LtGen Ante Roso, MajGen Milivoj Petkovic, and finally MajGen Tihomir Blaskic – all except Blaskic being seconded Croatian Army (HV) officers.

Table 4: Battle Order of Croatian Defence Council, May 1992–Dec 1993

GHQ, Mostar

(*Brigadir* Milivoj Petkovic; 24.7.1993 *General-bojnik* Slobodan Praljak; 12.11.1993 *General-pukovnik* Ante Roso)
'Ante Bruno Busic' Rgt (Capljina) – three bns & smaller units throughout 1–3 OPGs
Special Purposes Unit 'Ludvig Pavlovic' (Capljina)
1 MP Bn (Mostar)

1 SE Herzegovina Operational Zone (Siroki Brijeg)

(*Pukovnik/ Brigadir* Miljenko Lasic, *Brigadir* Filip Filipovic)
1 Herzegovina Bde 'Prince Domagoj' (Capljina); 2 Herzegovina Bde, 1 MP Lt Assault Bn 'Jure and Boban' & 3 (later 5) MP Bn (Mostar); 3 Herzegovina Bde (Mostar-Krusevo); 4 Herzegovina Bde 'Stjepan Radic' (Ljubuski-Grude-Citluk); 6 Bde 'Knight Ranko Boban' (Grude); 7 Bde 'Mario Hrkac Cikota' & 'Ivica Jelcic-Carls' Bn/ 'A.B. Busic' Rgt (Siroki Brijeg); 'Prince Branimir' Bde (Citluk); 'Duke Stjepan' Bde (Konjic)

2 NW Herzegovina OZ (Tomislavgrad)

(*Pukovnik* Zeljko Siljeg, *Brigadir* Ivan Peric, *Brigadir* Josip Cerni)
'King Tomislav' Bde (Tomislavgrad); 'Petar Kresimir IV' Bde, 'Ferdo Sucic' Bn/ 'A.B.Busic' Rgt, 2 MP Lt Assault Bn & (later 6) MP Bn (Livno); 'Rama' Bde (Prozor); 'Dr Ante Starcevic' Bde & 'Zvonko Krajina' Bn /'A.B.Busic' Rgt (Uskoplje); 'Eugen Kvaternik' Bde (Bugojno); 'Hrvoje Vukcic Hrvatinic' Bde

(Jajce, based Tomislavgrad); 5 Bde & 'Knight Damir Martic' Bn/ 'A.B.Busic' Rgt (Posusje)

3 Central Bosnia OZ (Vitez)

(Mihovil Strujic, *Pukovnik/brigadir* Tihomir Blaskic)
4 (later 7) MP Bn (Travnik); 3 MP Lt Assault Bn (Vitez); 4 Lt AA Miss Bn (Novi Travnik); Arty Unit; AA Unit
1 OPG: Travnik & 'Frankopan' Bdes (Travnik); 'Stjepan Tomasevic' Bde (Novi Travnik); Vitez Bde (Vitez); 'Jure Francetic' Bde (Zenica)
2 OPG: 'Ban Jelacic' Bde (Kiseljak-Kresevo); 'Nikola Subic Zrinski' Bde (Busovaca); 'Kotromanic' Bde (Kakanj); 'Bobovac' Bde (Vares)
3 OPG: 110 'Usora' Bde (Tesanj-Zabljak); 111 'Xp' Bde & 'Andrija Tadic' Bn (Zepce); 'Komusina' Ind Bn (Komusina)
Independent: 'King Tvrtko' Bde (Sarajevo); 115 'Zrinski' Bde (Tuzla-Drijenca)

4 Bosnian Posavina OPG (Jan 1993, OZ) (Orasje)

101 Bde (Bosanski Brod); 102 Bde (Odzak); 103 Bde (Derventa); 104 Bde (Bosanski Samac); 105 Bde (Modrica); 106 Bde, 4 MP Lt Assault Bn & 5 (later 8) MP Bn (Orasje); 107 Bde (Gradacac); 108 Bde (Brcko); 109 Bde (Doboj)

GHQ Bihac Area

101 Bn (Bihac)

The HVO followed the HV organization. The 50,000-strong force (including seconded HV personnel) comprised GHQ at Mostar, and four corps-status 'operational zones': 1 OZ (SE Herzegovina), 2 OZ (NW Herzegovina), 3 OZ (central Bosnia), and 4 OZ (Posavina). There was also an HVO headquarters in the Bihac enclave, liaising with ABiH 5 Corps. Each OZ controlled 8–14 infantry brigades, an MP battalion and an MP light assault battalion. The HVO also included the élite Ante Bruno Busic Rgt manned by professional soldiers; two independent infantry battalions, a light AA battalion, and special forces and artillery units.

There were 38 infantry brigades formed by reservists – 19 with names and/or numbers, and 19 with names only. The names commemorated figures from Croatian and Bosnian history, such as Tvrtko Kotromanic, King of Bosnia (1180–1204); Josip Jelacic (1801–1859), Governor of Croatia; Ante Bruno Busic (1939–78), a prominent emigré Croat; and,

An HVO private, in camouflage uniform with an M92 HVO left sleeve badge, standing in front of a home-made armoured vehicle in Livno, western Herzegovina, August 1992. The Croats were particularly skilled in converting commercial vehicles into effective armour. (Davor Marijan)

Table 5:
Battle Order of Croatian Defence Council, Dec 1993–Oct 1995

GHQ (Mostar)

(*General-pukovnik* Ante Roso; 26.4.1994
General-bojnik Milivoj Petkovic; 5.8.1995
General-bojnik Tihomir Blaskic)
60 Cdo Guard Bn 'Ludvig Pavlovic' & Training Centre (Capljina); MP Lt Assault Bde & 1 MP Bn (Mostar); Eng Bn; 71 Sig Coy, 154 Log Unit

Corps Region Mostar

1 'Ante Bruno Busic' & 2 Gds Mot Bdes & 50 HDR 'Prince Domagoj' (Capljina); 56 HDR 'Duke Stjepan' (Konjic, based Capljina); 81 HDR (Mostar); 82 HDR (Mostar-Krusevo); 83 HDR 'Mario Hrkac Cikota' (Siroki Brijeg); 'Stjepan Radic' HDR (Ljubuski); 40 HDR 'Knight Ranko Boban' (Grude); 41 HDR 'Prince Branimir' (Citluk)

Corps Region Tomislavgrad

1 HDR (Posusje); 55 HDR (Kupres); 79 HDR 'King Tomislav' (Tomislavgrad); 80 HDR 'Petar

Kresimir IV' (Livno); 97 HDR 'Hrvoje Vukcic Hrvatinic' (Jajce, based Tomislavgrad); 42 HDR 'Rama' (Prozor); 43 HDB 'Dr Ante Starcevic' (Uskoplje)

Corps Region Vitez

3 Gds Mot Bde 'Hawks' (Vitez); 90 HDR (Novi Travnik); 91 HDR (Travnik); 92 HDR 'Viteska' (Vitez); 93 HDR 'Nikola Subic Zrinski' (Busovaca;) 94 HDR (Kiseljak); 95 HDR 'Marinko Bosnjak' (Kresevo); 96 HDR 'Bobovac' (Vares); 110 HDR 'Usora' (Tesanj-Zabljak); 111 HDR 'Xp' (Zepce); 44 HDB 'Jure Francetic' (Zenica); 45 HDB 'Komusina' (Komusina)

Corps Region Orasje

4 Gds Mot Bde 'Sons of Posavina', 106, 201 & 202 HDR & 162 Log Base (Orasje)

GHQ Bihac Region (summer 1995, Bihac Corps Area)

101 HDR 'Ante Knezevic-Krle' (Bihac)

A T-55 tank of the HVO's 1 Guards Brigade, finished in a four-colour 'splotchy' camouflage scheme, with white tactical numbers on the glacis and turret sides and gold-on-black insignia on the turret cheeks. The crew are wearing ex-JNA black cloth reinforced tank helmets, a copy of the Soviet pattern; the brigade's beret was black, with a badge of the Croatian chequered shield on a gold disc. (Davor Marijan)

controversially, Jure Francetic (1912–42), commander of the infamous Ustasha 'Black Legion'. Each *brigada* had 3–4 battalions and supporting services. By the end of 1992 or early 1993 the majority-Moslem 107 & 109 Bdes (designated Moslem-Croat Defence Council – MHVO) were transferred to the ABiH as 107 'Chivalrous' Mot Bde and 109 Mtn Bde respectively; the 70 per cent Moslem contingent in 108 Bde also left, to form the ABiH 108 Mot Bde.

In Nov 1993 HV Gen Ante Roso took over command and reorganized the HVO following the revised HV model. The four OZs were redesignated Corps Districts Mostar, Tomislavgrad, Vitez and Orasje (the latter comprising the drastically reduced Bosanska Posavina). Four élite Guards Motorized Brigades were formed, each *motorizirana brigada* comprising professional troops. Twenty-nine brigades (1, 40–44, 50, 55, 56, 79–83, 90–97, 101, 106–108, 201, 202 & Stjepan Radic) were re-formed as Home Defence Rgts, usually with the same name and depot; each HDR (*domobranska pukovnija*) had three infantry battalions. Four brigades were disbanded, and the MP element was reduced to one light assault brigade at Mostar.

Eight HVO units served with the ABiH. Following the outbreak of the Moslem-Croat armed conflict on 17 Aug 1992, the HVO collaborated with the Bosnian-Serbs and fought ABiH forces around Sarajevo, in central Bosnia and in W Herzegovina; however, the Moslem-Croatian alliance survived in Orasje (Posavina), Usora (central Bosnia) and Bihac (NW Bosnia). At the same time two HVO brigades were forcibly incorporated into the ABiH: 115 Bde in Nov 1993, into ABiH 2 Corps, followed in Dec by the King Tvrtko Bde into 1 Corps.

Bosnian HOS personnel on parade in 1992. The men in the foreground are wearing black HOS berets, field tunics and trousers, while those in the background have US Army-pattern camouflage peaked field caps and field uniforms.

Other Bosnian-Croat forces

The embryonic Croatian Air Force was unable to spare many aircraft for its HVO ally, but initially GHQ Mostar operated two civil aircraft with 12 personnel. Later the HVO AF & AA Artillery was formed, with 11 Combined Sqn operating helicopters and transport aircraft, 121 Observation Bn (Ljubuski) and 14 AA Missile Unit. There were no naval forces. The Bosnian-Croat Police operated in Herceg Bosna's 30 districts, wearing Croatian Police uniforms with Herceg Bosna cap and sleeve insignia.

Herceg Bosna police on parade, 1993. They wear dark blue Croatian Police M91 uniforms with translucent white plastic cap and sleeve covers, and Herceg Bosna cap, sleeve and breast badges.

Croatian Defence Forces

The Croatian Defence Forces (HOS), formed in June 1991 under the extreme nationalist Croatian Party of Rights (HSP), was disbanded by the Croatian government on 21 Dec 1991. However, the commander MajGen Blaz Kraljevic, and some diehard personnel organized a new HOS in Bosnia which, in May 1992, became an official component of the OSRBiH. The HOS comprised about 5,000 Bosnian-Croats, foreign volunteers, and Bosnian-Moslems (about 30 per cent of the total), wearing distinctive black uniforms with some World War II NDH-pattern insignia. The HOS, including its Black Legion (*Crna legija*) unit, gained a reputation for bravery when fighting in Bosanski Brod, Konjic, Mostar, Novi Travnik and Zenica districts, but also for atrocities against Bosnian-Serb civilians. Kraljevic defied Croatian government policy by advocating a Bosnian-Croat alliance, and on 2 Aug 1992 he was killed in a firefight with HVO military police at a Mostar checkpoint. On 21 Aug the HOS disbanded, its personnel joining the HVO or ABiH.

Croatian Army

From May 1992 some Croatian Army (HV) personnel fought in HVO units as official allies of the Bosnian armed forces in W Herzegovina and Posavina. HV advice, equipment and manpower transformed the HVO into the most effective military force in Bosnia.

THE WAR IN BOSNIA-HERZEGOVINA

The Bosnian War lasted almost four years, from 1 Nov 1991 until the enduring ceasefire of 12 Oct 1995. It was essentially a brutal civil war, but the involvement of Croatia and the rump of Yugoslavia internationalized the conflict, leading to United Nations intervention enforced by NATO.

The UN passed five measures in hope of mitigating the effects of the war: on 25 Sept 1991 an arms embargo was applied to all Yugoslav republics; on 14 Sept 1992 UN Protection Force (UNPROFOR) troops totalling 39,490 were sent to Bosnian-Moslem and Bosnian-Croat areas; on 9 Oct 1992 a No-Fly Zone was declared, enforced from 12 Apr 1993 by NATO in Operation 'Deny Flight'; on 16 Nov 1992, border controls were ordered to prevent Croatian and Yugoslavian intervention; and on 6 May 1993 Sarajevo, Bihac, Gorazde, Srebrenica, Tuzla and Zepa were declared 'safe areas' supposedly under UNPROFOR protection.

There were also five unsuccessful international peace negotiations between Sept 1991 and 29 Nov 1993. Eventually, US-brokered negotiations led on 31 May 1994 to the partition of Bosnia into the Moslem-Croat Federation of Bosnia-Herzegovina (51 per cent of the territory) and *Republika Srpska* (49 per cent). On 30 Aug 1995, NATO began air-strikes on VRS positions to drive *Republika Srpska* to the negotiating table. A ceasefire was called on 12 Oct 1995, leading to the Dayton Agreement of 14 Dec and the end of the war.

Until 1995 the war was relatively static, with the three armies defending, consolidating and gingerly expanding their existing territory, often resorting to forced evacuation and even to murder of 'enemy' minorities – infamously defined as 'ethnic cleansing'.

Bosnian-Croat HVO troops meet amid the rubble in the outskirts of Mostar, late June 1992, after the joint HVO-ABiH offensive which forced VRS 6 Corps back into eastern Herzegovina. At right, wearing an M92 black beret and Police breast badge, is a military policeman from 1 MP Bn; MP units were always stationed at Mostar, the Bosnian-Croat GHQ. The police of all communities provided an important source of disciplined manpower and became more or less absorbed into the military, sometimes forming élite units. In what was essentially a civil war fought by rapidly formed and sketchily trained forces, the need for reliable personnel to enforce order was also a factor. (Imperial War Museum)

Siege of Sarajevo, 5 April 1992–12 October 1995

Sarajevo suffered the longest siege in modern history, which dominated the international media and often overshadowed fighting elsewhere. JNA Sarajevo Corps and Bosnian-Serb units (later VRS 4 Sarajevo-Romanija Corps) in the western suburbs and northern and southern hills besieged the Sarajevo TO (later ABiH 1 Corps) defending the Moslem Old Town and the ethnically mixed Centre, New Town and Hadzici districts in the Miljacka valley, and also high ground including Zuc Hill and Mount Igman – the garrison's only avenue of contact with other ABiH forces. The smaller but better-armed Bosnian-Serb force under Gen Ratko Mladic blockaded food, medical, electricity, water and heating supplies, and shelled, mortared and sniped at the more numerous but poorly armed ABiH troops (and civilians), trapping the Bosnian Presidency government.

On 2 May 1992 the JNA captured President Izetbegovic at Sarajevo Airport, and exchanged him for Gen Kukanjac, the captured JNA Sarajevo Corps commander. Meanwhile relief attempts by Bosnian-Moslem troops in Visoko in the north-west were prevented by the HVO's 2 OPG at Kiseljak. On 30 May VRS shells hit a bread queue causing 120 civilian casualties; and fighting and bombardment were heaviest from July 1992 to May 1993. On 6 June 1992 the JNA evacuated the city, and on 8 June the UN began airlifting food and medicine to the airport, ceremonially 'opened' by French President Mitterrand on 28 June. (During the ABiH-HVO confrontation there were clashes at Stup, western Sarajevo, on 17 Aug 1992; and on 4 Nov 1993 the ABiH expelled HVO 3 OZ troops from Vares district, north of the city.)

A Bosnian soldier patrols the streets of Sarajevo while a little girl looks out from her shattered window during the street fighting in July 1992. He wears a US camouflage uniform and body armour, with an M92 ABiH metal cap badge and cloth sleeve shield, both incorporating the Bosnian coast of arms. The following month a new ABiH left sleeve shield would be authorized. On a green, round-bottomed shield edged yellow, the coat-of-arms in smaller size was set on crossed swords, below yellow script 'ARMIJA/ REPUBLIKE/ BOSNE I HERCEGOVINE' – see Plate B.
© Corbis

23

Close-up of a Bosnian-Moslem policeman in eastern Mostar, 1993. He is wearing a greenish-brown summer shirt with the District of Mostar shoulder title – 'CSB/Mostar' (for *centar sluzbi bezbjednosti*), above a Bosnian Police sleeve shield. Both badges are in black cloth, edged yellow, with white inscriptions and devices.

On 4 Aug 1993 the Bosnian-Serb VRS sealed off Sarajevo by capturing Mts Igman and Bjelasnica, but NATO troops forced a withdrawal on 15 Aug. Units functioning as private armies existed across Bosnia; on 26 Oct 1993, ABiH 9 Mtn Bde (Ramiz Delalic-Celo) and 10 Mot Bde (Musan Topalovic-Caco) were defeated in gun-battles in Sarajevo by 3,000 ABiH troops and Bosnian Police.

On 5 Feb 1994 68 people were killed and 200 wounded by shelling in the infamous Markale Market massacre, after which NATO forced the VRS to withdraw their heavy artillery. On 6 Oct 1994 the rearmed ABiH 1 Corps entered the Mt Igman demilitarized zone to attack the VRS, but retreated under threat of NATO air-strikes. During Oct and Nov 1994 the ABiH advanced south of Sarajevo, although VRS 4 Corps prevented ABiH 2 Corps from relieving the city in June–July 1995. The city's heating, electricity and water were restored, and on 12 Oct 1995 a ceasefire was called. Sarajevo, with 526,000 inhabitants, had suffered some 12,000 dead and 35,000 buildings destroyed, and had shrunk to a population of about 250,000; but it had survived.

Eastern Bosnia, 3 March 1992–25 July 1995

This campaign was the most vicious of the war, as VRS 3 & 4 Corps, later joined by 5 Corps – and supported by Serb militias and the JNA/ VJ Nis and Uzice Corps from Serbia – 'ethnically cleansed' the region. On 3 Mar 1992 Serb militias attacked Gorazde, and then key towns on the Drina River frontier. Bijeljina was occupied 1–4 Apr 1992, Zvornik 8–10 Apr, Visegrad 13 Apr, and Foca in May. Most of E Bosnia was now in Bosnian-Serb hands, leaving Tuzla as the only major town held by the Bosnian TO. The Bosnian-Moslems also clung desperately to the Srebrenica, Zepa and Gorazde enclaves, swollen by panic-stricken refugees and surrounded by hostile VRS forces.

In 1994 Gen Mladic decided to attack the UN so-called 'safe areas'. On 7 Apr 4 Corps attacked Gorazde, held by ABiH 1 Gorazde Bde, but in retaliation NATO attacked VRS positions on 10–11 April; on 23 Apr the Bosnian-Serbs withdrew, and later ABiH 2 Corps managed to force a corridor to Gorazde from central Bosnia, ensuring the town's survival.

On 11 July the VRS attacked and occupied Srebrenica, meeting minimal resistance from ABiH 28 Div and none from a Dutch UN battalion. The subsequent VRS massacre of more than 7,000 Bosnian-Moslem male civilians horrified the world, and earned Gen Mladic international condemnation. In spite of NATO threats the VRS occupied Zepa on 25 July, brushing aside ABiH 101 Bde and the Ukrainian UN battalion.

Posavina Corridor, 15 March–8 October 1992

The Posavina Corridor in N Bosnia comprised the mainly Serb Modrica, the mainly Croat Odzak, and the mainly Moslem Brcko. It was held by the HV and HVO 4 OZ to the north and ABiH 2 Corps to the south, facing attacks from VRS 1 Corps in the west and 3 Corps from the east. The VRS's determination to create a secure link between Bosnian Krajina and E Bosnia led to some of the fiercest fighting of the war.

On 3 Mar 1992 Serb militias and Bosnian-Serb TO attacked Bosanski Brod, held by a scratch formation of PL, armed HDZBiH volunteers and local police, before HVO units were formed on 11 May 1992. On 25 Mar the Serbs and Bosnian-Serbs fired 2,000 missiles at the beleaguered town. The emboldened VRS advanced, taking Derventa on 8 July and Bosanski Brod on 7 Oct, occupying N Bosnia and creating a tenuous link – in some places only 3 miles wide. The Orasje Pocket, however, remained in HVO hands, and southern Brcko and southern Gradacac districts under ABiH 2 Corps, creating a stalemate until 12 Oct 1995.

Central Bosnia, 2 May 1992–12 September 1995

This Bosnian-Moslem heartland, defended by two ABiH corps, was threatened by both Serbs and Croats. In the north, ABiH 2 Corps faced VRS 1 Corps to their west and 3 Corps to their east; in the south, ABiH 3 Corps confronted VRS 1 Corps to their west, 4 & 5 Corps to their east, HVO 1 & 2 OZ to their south, and Bosnian-Croat enclaves held by 3 OZ.

On 2 May 1992 JNA Banja Luka Corps captured Doboj; and on 20 Jun, before the Moslem-Croat conflict officially commenced, HVO and TORBiH units clashed at Novi Travnik. In Oct, 7 Moslem Mtn Bde formed at Zenica with *Mujahedin* who were hostile to local civilians (including insufficiently religious Bosnian-Moslems). On 18 Oct ABiH and HVO units clashed at Vitez and again at Novi Travnik; on 25 Oct the HVO captured Prozor, but disputes between ABiH and HVO units defending Jajce allowed VRS 1 Corps to capture the town on 29 Oct – although the ABiH held Maglaj from VRS 1 Corps on 13 Dec, thereby saving the north-west sector.

On 16 Apr 1993 HVO troops killed about 116 Moslem civilians at Ahmici near Vitez, earning the HVO 3 OZ commander, Brig Tihomir Blaskic, an indictment from the International Criminal Tribunal for

General-potpukovnik **Stanislav Gavric (left), commanding the VRS 4 Sarajevo-Romanija Corps besieging Sarajevo, with his bodyguard (right) after talks with UN commanders in February 1994. Gavric wears the distinctive M92 Serbian officers' field cap with the two thin and one medium gold braids of colonel-general's rank. The two officers' field jackets and armour vests show different camouflage patterns.**

Former Yugoslavia (ICTY). The ABiH 3 Corps expelled the HVO from Travnik on 7 Jun, only to lose Trnovo, south of Sarajevo, to VRS 4 Corps. ABiH units killed about 19 Bosnian-Croat civilians at Uzdol near Prozor on 14 Sept 1993, while the HVO massacred some 80 Bosnian-Moslems at Stupni Do near Vares. Now ABiH 3 Corps counter-attacked in strength, taking Vares from the HVO on 4 November.

The central Bosnian front then fell relatively dormant until 28 Mar 1995, when ABiH 3 Corps captured Mt Vlasic, north of Travnik, forcing VRS 1 Corps back towards Jajce. On 12 Sept, as part of the joint Croat-Moslem 1995 offensive, ABiH 3 Corps took Donji Vakuf.

Herzegovina, 1 November 1991–18 August 1995

Herzegovina was divided into the west, dominated by Bosnian-Croats, capital Mostar, defended by HVO 2 OZ and ABiH 4 Corps in the east and HVO 1 OZ in the west; and eastern Herzegovina, capital Trebinje, which was part of *Republika Srpska* and defended by VRS 6 Corps.

In Mar 1992 JNA Trebinje-Bilec OPG advanced eastwards, attacking Capljina district on 7 Mar, Neum (Bosnia's Adriatic port) on 19 Mar, and Mostar on 3 April. On 8 Apr other JNA units took Kupres, occupied by the Bosnian-Croat HOS on 3 April. On 16 June, HVO 1 OZ with TORBiH Mostar Bn counter-attacked east of Mostar, forcing VRS 6 Corps back into E Herzegovina, but were ordered by Croatian President Tudjman not to take Trebinje.

This front fell quiet until 9 May 1993 during the Moslem-Croat confrontation, when HV and HVO 1 OZ forces, observing a local

Ratko Mladic, now a *general-pukovnik*, attempts to enthuse a rather dispirited group of *Republika Srpska* troops besieging the Bihac Pocket in December 1994.

ceasefire with the VRS, attacked the ABiH, occupied eastern Mostar and imprisoned the Bosnian-Moslem inhabitants in the Heliodrom (Mostar), Dretelj, Gabela and Ljubuski camps. In June 1993 ABiH 6 Corps formed for Operation 'Neretva 93' – the destruction of the HVO in W Herzegovina; but the understrength corps failed to defeat the determined and well-equipped Bosnian-Croats. The ABiH killed 35 Bosnian-Croat civilians at Grabovica near Mostar, and the HVO retaliated, destroying the world-famous Ottoman 'Old Bridge' at Mostar.

The front then fell silent again until 18 Aug 1995, when HV and HVO 1 OZ advanced towards Trebinje again, before signing a local ceasefire with VRS 6 Corps.

The Bihac Pocket, 21 April 1992–12 October 1995

The Bihac Pocket in NW Bosnia comprised the four largely Bosnian-Moslem districts of Velika Kladusa, Cazin, Bihac and Bosanska Krupa, defended by ABiH Una-Sana OPG (later 5 Corps), and HVO 101 Bn. This region faced the 15, 21 and 39 Corps of the Serbian Krajina Army (SVK) in Serbian Krajina (RSK), VRS 1 Corps to the east and 2 Corps to the south. Although surrounded by hostile Croatian-Serb and Bosnian-Serb forces, the determined Bosnian-Moslem defenders held the 200-mile perimeter and mounted local counter-attacks in July, Sept, Oct and Nov 1992, and Jan and Apr 1993.

Fikret 'Babo' ('Dad') Abdic, a popular Moslem SDA minister and industrialist, later rejected President Izetbegovic's policies as excessively anti-Serb, and on 27 Sept 1993 he proclaimed himself president of the Autonomous Province of Western Bosnia, in Velika Kladusa and Cazin districts. He established a People's Defence Force (*Narodna odbrana Autonomne Pokrajine Zapadna Bosna* – NO) commanded by Asim Delic, with six NO brigades formed from ABiH 5 Corps' 521 & 527 Mtn Bdes: 1 Bde (Velika Kladusa), 2 Bde (Marjanovci), 3 Bde, 4 Bde (Pecigrad), 5 Bde (Kudici-Liskovac) and 6 Bde (Trzac). However, ABiH 5 Corps, from Nov 1993 commanded by the talented Brig Atif Dudakovic, attacked the NO and occupied Velika Kladusa on 21 Aug 1994, forcing Abdic, the NO and 20,000 civilians to flee to Serbian Krajina. 5 Corps then blocked a counter-attack on 12 Sept by NO brigades, SVK 39 Corps and VRS 1 & 2 Corps; and in Operation 'Grmec 94' they forced VRS 2 Corps back from Bihac town.

The NO, now under Serif Mustedanagic, was re-equipped by the SVK and reorganized into three brigades (1–3). On 4 Nov 1994 the NO, SVK and VRS invaded the Bihac Pocket. The HV stood ready to intervene to save ABiH 5 Corps, but the invasion was halted on 23 Nov by a NATO attack on three VRS missile sites. Nevertheless, on 17 Dec 1994 Abdic and his allies recaptured Velika Kladusa district. On 26 July 1995 Abdic proclaimed the Republic of Western Bosnia, but on 7 Aug the ABiH 5 Corps recaptured Velika Kladusa and linked up with HV forces advancing through Serbian Krajina under Operation 'Storm', relieving the Bihac Pocket.

The NO and Abdic's mini-state collapsed; HV forces and 5 Corps advanced eastwards in Sept 1995, retaking Bosanska Krupa district and capturing Bosanski Petrovac and Sanski Most from VRS 1 Corps, and were advancing on Prijedor when the 12 Oct ceasefire was announced. Abdic fled to President Tudjman's protection in Croatia, but following Tudjman's death he was tried in 2002 by a Croatian court and sentenced to 20 years imprisonment.

Western Bosnia, 4 April 1992–12 October 1995

Western Bosnia was the *Republika Srpska* heartland, containing the de facto capital, Banja Luka. It was defended by the strong VRS 1 Corps and 2 Corps in SW Bosnia, but was scarcely threatened at all, being bordered by friendly Serbian Krajina, and with hostile Croatia and Bosnian-Moslem central Bosnia too preoccupied with their own survival. Thus the Bosnian-Serbs consolidated their hegemony in the region.

On 4 Apr 1992 JNA Banja Luka Corps seized Banja Luka town, and on 2 May killed or expelled the local Bosnian-Croats, Moslems and other minorities, destroying villages, mosques and Catholic churches in Banja Luka and Prijedor districts. They also established the notorious Manjaca, Keraterm, Trnopolje and Omarska internment camps. Meanwhile, 1 Corps secured the Posavina Corridor and attacked central Bosnia, taking Doboj on 2 May and Jacje on 29 Oct 1992; they also attacked the Bihac Pocket, while 2 Corps confronted the HVO 2 OZ.

By 1995 the HVO and ABiH had been re-equipped. On 28 Mar 1995 ABiH 3 Corps forced 1 Krajina Corps back towards Jajce, and on 29 July

Serb militiaman wearing the traditional *sajkaca* cap, with a privately bought brass badge showing the double-headed eagle in a wreath. This headgear was favoured by the Serbian Chetnik Movement (*Srpski cetnicki pokret* – SCP), which was active in Nevesinje, Kupres, Derventa, Modrica and Tuzla districts in 1992, and Kalinovik and Maglaj districts in 1993. (See also Elite 138, Plate C1.)

HV forces and HVO 2 OZ took Bosansko Grahovo and Glamoc from the demoralized 2 Krajina Corps. Some 100,000 Bosnian-Serb and Croatian-Serb civilians streamed towards Serbia to escape the Croatian steamroller. Following the end of this Operation 'Storm' on 10 Aug, the HV, HVO and ABiH continued advancing; by 12 Sept the 2 Corps region had been overrun – Bosanski Petrovac and eastern Prijedor by ABiH 5 Corps; Drvar, Kljuc and western Banja Luka by the HV; and Kupres and Jajce by HVO 2 OZ – while in the 1 Corps region ABiH 5 Corps occupied Sanski Most, and 3 Corps, Donji Vakuf.

The Bosnian-Serb VRS retaliated by expelling the remaining 20,000 Bosnian-Moslems and -Croats from Bosnian Krajina, and on 19 Sept 1995 blocked an HV pincer movement from Croatian W Slavonia against Bosanska Dubica District. On 10 Oct, two days before the Dayton ceasefire, the HV and ABiH 5 Corps foiled a desperate VRS 1 Corps counter-attack towards Kljuc and Bosanska Krupa; on the same day the HV and HVO entered Mrkonjic Grad, and 5 Corps captured Sanski Most.

A member of the anti-tank battalion of the HVO's 1 Guards Brigade preparing to fire an AT missile launcher. Note that he is wearing his unit badge on the left upper sleeve of his camouflage winter field jacket – the right arm was the normal position. The oval patch is black with yellow script between double yellow borders, and a three-quarter view of a tank in the centre. (Davor Marijan)

Bosnian aftermath

The Dayton Agreement of 14 Dec 1995 ended the Bosnian War. Bosnia became one state, divided approximately along the 12 Oct 1995 ceasefire line into two 'entities'. These were the Bosnian-Croat Federation (capital Sarajevo) with ten Moslem, Croat and mixed cantons in NW, SW, central and E Bosnia, Sarajevo and W Herzegovina; and *Republika Srpska* (capital also Sarajevo), of seven regions with 63 districts in W, N and E Bosnia and E Herzegovina.

A private of the HVO 1 Guards Brigade wearing an obsolete US Army helmet, and the badge of the élite 'Ante Bruno Busic' Rgt on his right sleeve. Within a red outer and narrow white inner borders, the black patch bears a large white '1' at the top, above the gold-trimmed Croatian chequered shield; centred on this is a black/white image of a man's face. Above, superimposed across the brigade numeral, is gold lettering 'GARDIJSKA BRIGADA'; and below, 'ANTE BRUNO BUSIC'. (Davor Marijan)

The Federation Armed Forces (*Vojska Federacije* – VF), GHQ Tuzla, had 24,000 regular and 15,000 reserve troops divided into the Bosnian-Moslem Component (VF-B) with 16,618 troops in ex-ABiH 1, 2 & 5 Corps; the ex-HVO Croatian Component (VF-H) with 7,225 in I Guards Corps; a joint Rapid Reaction Bde, and a joint Air Force. The VRS had 10,000 troops in 1, 3, 5 & 7 (ex-6) Corps and an air force. All 'corps' were actually of brigade size, divided into battalion-sized 'brigades'. On 1 Jan 2006, the VF and VRS were unified as the Armed Forces of Bosnia-Herzegovina (*Oruzane snage Bosne i Hercegovine* – OS BiH).

Bosnia remains under a UN administration, committed to establishing an independent republic with unified military and police forces. Initially this was supported by the NATO Implementation Force (IFOR) with 54,000 troops, divided into Multinational Divisions North, Southwest and Southeast. On 21 Dec 1996 the NATO Stabilization Force (SFOR) succeeded IFOR, with about 12,000 troops in multinational divisions (from late 2002, brigades). On 2 December 2004 the European Union Force (EUFOR) took over, with 2,000 troops in three multinational task forces – MTF North, Northwest (ex–SFOR Southwest) and Southeast.

KOSOVO

Kosovo (*Kosova* or *Kosovë* in Albanian) is a region in SW Serbia, representing 12 per cent of Serbian territory. In 1991 the population of 1,956,196 were 82 per cent Albanians, 11 per cent Serbs and Montenegrins, 3 per cent 'Gorani' Moslem-Serbs, 2 per cent Roma gypsies and 2 per cent other minorities. Kosovo-Albanians are predominantly Moslems, speaking a distinct Indo-european language written in the Latin alphabet.

On 28 June 1389 the Serbian Prince Lazar was defeated by the Ottoman Turks at the battle of Kosovo Polje ('Field of Blackbirds') near

President Milosevic appointed Dragoljub Ojdanic as VJ chief-of-staff in November 1998, as a more pliable officer than his predecessor, Gen Perisic; but only 15 months later he replaced him with Gen Nebojsa Pavkovic. Ojdanic wears the JNA/VJ M63 dark blue ceremonial uniform with the four-star insignia of a *general armije*; he was one of only a few officers to hold this rank.

General-pukovnik Nebojsa Pavkovic is shown here wearing the greyish-green M55 JNA/VJ service tunic, with general officers' gold braid M64 collar patches and M55 shoulder straps. The woven M92 armed forces badge is just visible on his left sleeve. Pavkovic commanded the Pristina Corps, then 3 Army during the Kosovo conflict; he succeeded Gen Ojdanic as chief-of-staff on 23 February 2000. Pavkovic switched allegiance from Milosevic to President Kostunica in October that year, but was dismissed in June 2002; in April 2005 he was indicted for war crimes at the International Criminal Tribunal.

Pristina, and Serbia began 428 years of Ottoman rule. The Serbs still regard Kosovo as the heartland of the Serbian state and Church, despite the dramatic alteration in the population balance. On 3 Sept 1945 Kosovo-Metohija became an Autonomous Region, and on 7 Apr 1963 an Autonomous Province of Serbia, within the Federal Republic of Yugoslavia. The Yugoslavian Communist regime discouraged Islam, but allowed the use of the Albanian language and some political freedom; on 21 Feb 1974 the province was awarded de facto republican status.

On 24 Apr 1987 Serbian President Slobodan Milosevic presented himself as an anti-Albanian Serb nationalist at a rally on the Kosovo Polje battlefield, and on 28 Mar 1989 he formally absorbed Kosovo into Serbia. In Dec 1989, Dr Ibrahim Rugova formed the moderate nationalist LDK party, and in June 1991 was elected president of the unofficial 'Kosova Republic', campaigning peacefully for UN recognition. Following the outbreak of the Bosnian War in Mar 1992, Milosevic unscrupulously accused the Bosnian-Moslems and Kosovar-Albanians of plotting 'holy war' against the Serbs, and in 1995 he deployed 25,000 Serb police to suppress the continuing unrest.

The Kosovo-Albanians had hoped that the Dayton Agreement would restore their autonomous status, but the international community shrank from further fragmentation of Yugoslavia. Rugova's pacifist policy was marginalized, and in 1996 the Kosovo Liberation Army (UÇK) began their guerrilla campaign.

Yugoslav Army

On 8 May 1992 the Yugoslav People's Army (JNA) became the Yugoslav Army (*Vojska Jugoslavije* – VJ); and on 20 May it officially evacuated Bosnia-Herzegovina, leaving four territorial corps and two OPG HQs to form the Bosnian-Serb VRS and Serbian Krajina SVK armies. A Special Forces Corps was established; Kumanovo Corps was renamed Leskovac Corps; and Bitola Corps, Sabac Corps, ex-Ljubljana troops and ex-Northern Theatre troops were disbanded. The May 1992 battle order comprised 1 Army in Vojvodina and northern Serbia, 2 Army in Montenegro and 3 Army in Kosovo and southern Serbia. Each army had HQ troops comprising a mixed artillery brigade and 1–4 Air Force AA missile regiments, with 2–7 corps and other major formations, totalling

(continued on page 41)

BOSNIAN-MOSLEM FORCES, 1992
1: Militiaman, Patriotic League, Sarajevo
2: Officer, Territorial Defence Force, Tuzla
3: *Samostalni inspektor*, Police Special Unit, Sarajevo

A

BOSNIA-HERZEGOVINA ARMY, 1992–93

1: *Vojnik*, winter 1992–93
2: Member of Special Units, 1992
3: *Mujahed*, 1993

B

BOSNIAN-MOSLEM FORCES, 1994–95
1: *Brigadni General*, ABiH; Sarajevo, 1994
2: *Nadkapetan*, 5 Corps; Bihac, 1995
3: *Vojnik*, NO; Velika Kladusa, 1995

C

D

BOSNIAN-CROAT FORCES, 1992–95
1: *Brigadir,* 1 Guards Bde, HVO, 1994
2: *Stozerni vodnik,* Military Police, HVO, 1995
3: *Porucnik,* HOS, 1992

1

2

3

E

ETHNIC ALBANIAN FORCES, 1999–2001
1: Officer, UÇK; Kosovo, 1999
2: Volunteer, UÇPMB; southern Serbia, 1999
3: Military Policeman, UÇK (NMET); Macedonia, 2001

F

YUGOSLAV & SERBIAN FORCES IN KOSOVO, 1999
1: *Porucnik*, Yugoslav Army
2: *Vodnik,* Serbian Special Police
3: Policeman, Serbian Special Operations Unit

G

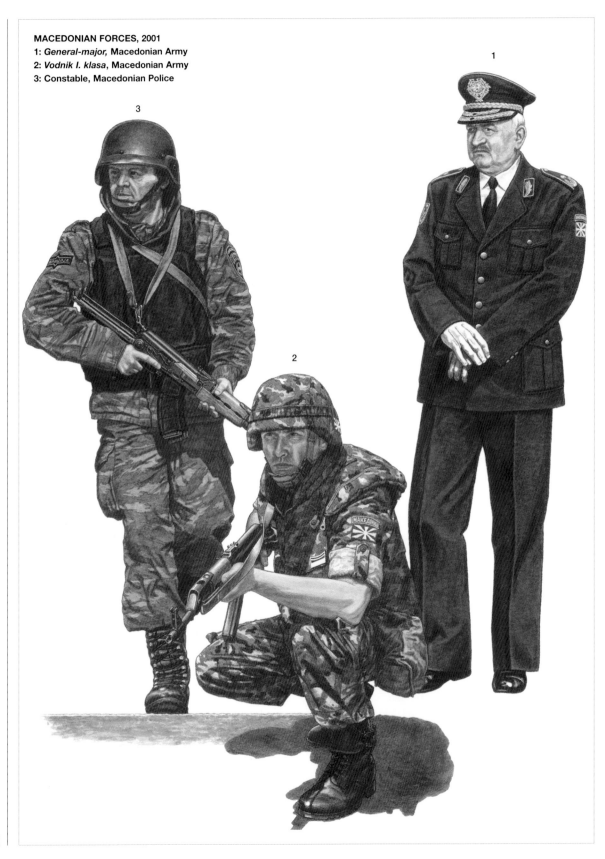

MACEDONIAN FORCES, 2001

1: *General-major,* Macedonian Army
2: *Vodnik I. klasa*, Macedonian Army
3: Constable, Macedonian Police

H

13. These major formations were the Special Forces and Mechanized Corps; the Novi Sad, Kragujevac, Podgorica, Uzice, Nis, Leskovac and Pristina territorial corps; the corps-sized Belgrade Defence Command and Timok Task Force; and the brigade-sized Danube and Drina Divisions. On 29 Aug 1993 Gen Momcilo Perisic took over command as VJ chief-of-staff but, uneasy over Milosevic's aggressive policy, he was replaced on 24 Nov 1998 by Gen Dragoljub Ojdanic, who was fully committed to a military solution in Kosovo.

The VJ in March 1999 had 101,657 troops from the remaining Yugoslav republics of Serbia and Montenegro. The May 1992 battle order of three armies and 13 major formations was retained. The Special Forces Corps grouped four élite armoured, motorized, parachute and special brigades, and the Mechanized Corps had five mechanized and mixed artillery brigades. A VJ territorial corps was much larger than its JNA predecessor, with about seven brigades: 0–2 armoured, 0–2 mechanized and light mechanized, 1–3 motorized and light motorized, 0–2 infantry and light infantry, 0–1 mixed artillery, and 0–1 mixed anti-tank. There were 77 brigades in all: 1 parachute, 1 special, 5 armoured, 8 mechanized, 23 motorized, 8 light motorized, 1 infantry, 12 light infantry, 2 light mountain, 10 mixed artillery, 1 mechanized AT and 5 mixed AT. Some were ex-Serbian and Montenegrin JNA brigades retaining JNA designations, and some new brigades formed from May 1992.

An armoured brigade had three armoured battalions with M84 or T-55 tanks; a mechanized brigade, 1–2 armoured and 1–3 mechanized battalions; a motorized brigade, three infantry battalions and an

Personnel of the Serbian State Security Department's Special Operations Unit (JSO) wearing black uniforms. Note the long black rectangular strip down both upper sleeves, with the white woven Cyrillic inscription 'POLICIJA' in vertical format.

A close-up of the JSO red beret and badge. These Serbian Special Police conducted numerous operations in Kosovo in 1998–99, in concert with Serbian militias, and using a variety of uniforms and weapons including NATO types. On the orders of their commander, Lukovic Ulemek, on 12 March 2003 a JSO operative named Zvezdan 'Zmija' ('Snake') Jovanovic assassinated the pro-Western reformist Serbian Prime Minister Zoran Djindjic, causing the JSO's instant disbandment.

armoured battalion. All three types of brigade HQ had an artillery battalion, MP company, reconnaissance company, AA battery and support units. A mixed artillery brigade had four battalions: howitzer, field artillery, multiple rocket-launcher and support. The 72 Special Bde included two élite counter-terrorist units: the Hawks *(Sokolovi)* Bn and Cobras *(Kobre)* Company. There were also independent engineer and signals regiments, MP battalions, and border battalions on the frontier with Albania.

The small Yugoslav Navy, based at Kotor (Montenegro) under ViceAdm Milan Zec, played no part in the Kosovo conflict, although it included the élite 82 Naval Commando Unit. The Yugoslav AF & AA Defence, under Gen Spasoje Smiljanic, was based in Zemun near Belgrade. It comprised the Air Corps (MajGen Radoljub Masic), with 172 Air Bde's four air regiments: 83 Fighter (attached to Pristina Corps), 204 Fighter, 98 Fighter-Bomber and 119 Helicopter, each divided into squadrons. The Air Defence Corps (MajGen Bransislav Petrovic) had missile regiments equipped with Soviet SAM-6s.

Yugoslav Interior Ministry forces

After 28 Feb 1990 the internal security of Vojvodina and Kosovo came under the Serbian Interior Ministry (*Ministarstvo Unutrasnjh Poslova* – MUP) in Belgrade, controlling the Serbian Police and Security Service.

The Serbian Police *(Milicija*, from 1996 *Policija)*, under Gen Djordjevic, was divided into 33 police secretariats – 19 in Serbia, 7 in Vojvodina and 7 in Kosovo. These secretariats were divided into police districts, each supervising a number of police stations. Kosovo-Albanian policemen were dismissed during the 1990s and replaced with Serbs.

The Serbian paramilitary Special Militia – from 3 Jan 1997, Special Police – Units *(Posebne jedinice milicije/ policije* – PJM/PJP) were commanded in 1998 by Gen Obrad Stevanovic, with 5,000 men divided into six brigades: 21 (Belgrade), 23 (Novi Sad), 24 (Pristina), 35 (Uzice), 36 (Kragujevac) and 37 (Nis). From that year they were extensively deployed in Kosovo; a 700-strong *brigada* was effectively a motorized light infantry battalion equipped with mortars, heavy machine-guns and APCs. There were also 8,000 reservists. PJP personnel wore a maroon beret with a badge of an oval Serbian shield in a wreath on a silver sword, and a camouflage field uniform with the cap badge device repeated as an embroidered left-sleeve shield. The Lightning *(Munja)* Platoon, with 30–50 PJP members, was established in 1998 by Nebojsa Minic for 'delicate' operations in Kosovo. The PJP were renamed Gendarmerie *(Zandarmerija)* on 28 June 2001.

These JSO personnel wear black face masks, with camouflage uniforms and US PASGT helmets. The distinctive left sleeve shield had a vertical sword motif on a light blue ground circled by a yellow wreath, on a white-bordered black shield with white Cyrillic script at the top.

The Special Counter-terrorist Unit (*Specijalna antiteroristicka jedinica* –
SAJ) was formed on 1 June 1992 and based in Belgrade; expanded from
400 to 1,000 strong for the Kosovo conflict, its élite platoons were
allocated to PJP brigades. The SAJ wore black berets and a metal
cap-badge depicting a Serbian shield on a silver two-headed eagle on a
gold sword, and black or camouflage field uniform with an embroidered
badge on the left upper sleeve. The Fog *(Magla)* OPG was formed in
Kosovo in late 1997 as part of the SAJ, operating 12- or 24-man assault
teams; they participated in massacres at Donje Prekaze, Racak and
Cuska. They usually wore black uniforms and favoured NATO weapons.
In June 2001 the SAJ was absorbed into the Gendarmerie.

The Serbian State Security Department (*Resor drzavne bezbednosti* –
RDB) was led by Gen Radomir 'Rade' Markovic. His deputy, Police
MajGen Curcic, ran plain-clothes intelligence and assassination
operatives from RDB's Gnjilane, Pristina and Prizren offices. Franko

Table 6: Battle Order of Yugoslav Army, March 1999

GHQ (Belgrade):

(*General-pukovnik* Dragoljub Ojdanic)
46 Security Mot Bde; Gds Bde

1 ARMY (Belgrade)

(*General-major* Srboljub Trajkovic)
152 Mix Arty Bde; 5 MP Bn; 149, 240, 310 & 401 AF SAM Rgts

Belgrade Defence Command: *reserve*, 151 Mot Bde; 153 & 505 Lt Mot Bdes; 150 Lt Mot Rgt; 22 Mix Arty Bde; 22 Mix AT Rgt; 585 AF Lt Inf Rgt

Special Forces Corps: 1 Armd Bde; Gds Mot Bde; 63 Para Bde; 72 Spec Bde; 25 MP Bn

Mechanized Corps: 1–3 Mech Bdes; 1 Mix Arty Bde; *reserve*, 35 Mech Bde

Novi Sad Corps: 36 Armd Bde; 12 & 453 Mech Bdes; 506 Inf Bde; 45 Lt Inf Bde; 16 Mix Arty Bdes; 16 Mix AT Bde; 2 MP Bn; *reserve*, 18 Mot Bde; 127 Lt Inf Bde

Kragujevac Corps: 51 Mech Bde; *reserve*, 80 & 130 Mot Bdes; 129 Lt Mot Bde; 20

& 21 Lt Inf Bdes; 24 Mix Arty Bde

Drina Div: 544 Mot Bde

Danube Div: *reserve*, 14 Lt Mot Bde

2 ARMY (Podgorica)

(Gen Martinovic; 1 Apr 1999 *General-major* Milorad Obradovic)
60 AF SAM Rgt

Podgorica Corps: 5 Mot Bde; 326 Mix Arty Bde; 56 Eng Rgt; 72 Border Bn; *reserve*, 57 & 179 Mot Bdes; 3 & 4 Lt Inf Bdes; 2 & 4 Lt Mtn Bdes

Uzice Corps: 37 Mot Bde; *reserve*, 168 Mot Bde; 27 Lt Mot Bde; 6, 7 & 134 Lt Inf Bde

3 ARMY (Nis)

(*General-pukovnik* Nebojsa Pavkovic)
150 & 202 (ex-2 Army HQ) Mix Arty Bdes; 7 & 311 AF SAM Rgts

Nis Corps: 211 Armd Bde; 4 Mot Bde; *reserve*, 2 & 805 Mot Bdes; 50 Lt Inf Bde; 203 Mix Arty Bde

Leskovac Corps: *reserve*, 89 & 135 Mot

Bdes; 21 & 42 Mix AT Bde

Pristina Corps: 52 MP Bn; 52 Eng Rgt; 52 Sig Rgt; 15 Armd Bde; 78, 125 & 549 Mot Bdes; 243 Mech Bde; 58, 175 & 354 Lt Inf Bdes; 52 Mix Arty Bde; 62 Mix AT Bde; 102 Mech AT Bde; 53, 55 & 57 Border Bns. *Reinforcements for Kosovo War from March 1999:* elements 63 Para & 72 Spec Bdes (Spec Forces); 13 Lt Mot Bde (Leskovac); 211 Armd Bde (Nis); elements 16 Mix Arty Bde (Novi Sad); 252 Armd, 37 Mot & 7 Lt Inf Bde (Uzice); various recon & MP units

Timok Task Force: 9 & 148 Mot Bdes; *reserve*, 23 & 35 Lt Inf Bdes

(**Note:** For comparison with earlier orbat, see Elite 138 *The Yugoslav Wars (1)*, page 9.)

Simatovic's Operations Department controlled the élite Special Operations Unit (*Jedinica za Specijalne Operacije* – JSO), formed by Simatovic in 1996 from the 'Red Berets' (see above, under 'Serb militias'). The JSO, under Milorad 'Legija' Lukovic Ulemek, comprised 400–500 assault troops mainly recruited from VJ Special Forces, and operating as 15- to 25-strong platoons in armoured vehicles. They armed, trained and co-ordinated the activities of Serb paramilitary militias, such as Dragoslav Bokan's White Eagles and the Vucjak Wolves – all of which operated in Kosovo, though more discreetly than in Croatia and Bosnia.

Kosovo Liberation Army

The *Ushtria Çlirimtare e Kosovës* (UÇK) was formed in 1992 by radical nationalist members of the Albanian minority in Macedonia, but soon moved to Kosovo to fill the vacuum created by Rugova's discredited pacifist policies. On 22 Apr 1996 the UÇK began offensive operations against the VJ and MUP forces. Membership until 1998 was only about 300, expanding in that year to some 7,000, and to about 17,000 by March 1999. These included activists from Kosovo and emigrés from Switzerland and Germany; about 300 ex-JNA personnel who had served in two Croatian Army battalions in the Croatian Homeland War; and a large number of part-time auxiliaries, all supported by funds from Albanian emigrés in the West. Initially the UÇK was commanded by Sylejman Selimi, replaced in May 1999 by Agim Çeku, a former JNA captain and Croatian Army *brigadir*.

In summer 1998 Rugova's prime minister in exile in Switzerland, Bujar Bukoshi, formed a rival force with Saudi Arabian support. This Kosovo Republic Armed Forces (*Forca e armatosura te Republikes se Kosovës* – FARK) was led by Ahmet Krasniqi; but in Sept 1998 the UÇK killed Krasniqi and absorbed his force. Agim Çeku reorganized the UÇK,

A parade of the VJ Guards Motorized Brigade, 1999. These Serbian troops are wearing the 'élite' maroon beret with the standard M92 cap badge, M92 left-sleeve badge and M91 camouflage uniforms – see Plate G. In 1999 the VJ was a formidable ethnic Serb military force, with the Vojvodina Hungarians as the only significant (though compliant) minority, fighting on short internal lines of supply, and determined to defend their historic homeland.

giving it a conventional military structure. Kosovo was divided into seven Operational Zones, each zone controlling 1–6 battalion-sized 'brigades' (111–171 series); 27 brigades have been identified. Officially each had 1,000 men in 20 companies each of 50–60 men, but most brigades were much smaller.

The OZs fought as independent units with minimal control from GHQ. Five Islamic groups served in the UÇK: the ABiH Black Swans; the 400-strong Albanian-American Atlantic Bde under Gami Shehu; a 120-man Iranian unit at Donji Prekaz; a Bosnian-Albanian unit led by an Egyptian, Abu Ismail; and *Mujahedin* from Afghanistan, Algeria, Chechnya, Egypt, Saudi Arabia and Sudan. The UÇK was trained by CIA and British SAS instructors at camps at Kukës, Tropojë and Bajram Curri in NE Albania and Labinot near Tirana. Initially it was armed with assault

Table 7: Battle Order of Kosovo Liberation Army, May 1999

GHQ, Kukës (NE Albania)

I Drenica Operational Zone (N-central Kosovo)

(Sami Lustaku)
111 'Fatmir Ibishi', 112 'Sherif Jonuzi', 113 'Mujë Krasniqi' & 114 'Fehmi Lladrovci' Bdes

II Llap OZ (NE Kosovo)

(Mustafa 'Remi' Rustem)
121 'Shaban Shala', 122 'Zahir Pajaziti', 123, 124 & 125 Bdes

III Rrafshi i Dukagjinit OZ (W Kosovo)

(Ramush Haradinaj)
131 'Jusuf Gërvalla', 132 'Myrtë Zeneli', 133 'Adrian Krasniqi', 134 'Bedri Shala', 136 & 137 Bdes

IV Shala ë Bajgores OZ (N Kosovo)

(Rahman Rama)
141 'Mehë Uka', 142 'Azem Galica' & 143 Bdes

V Pashtriku OZ (S-central Kosovo)

(Tahir 'Drini' Sinani)
151 'Zahir Pajaziti', 152 ' Shala' & 153 Bdes

VI Nerodime OZ (E Kosovo)

(Shukri Buja)
161 'Ahmet Kaqiku', 162 'Agim Bajrami' & 163 Bdes

VII Kara Dagh OZ (S Kosovo)

171 'Kadri Zeka', 172 & 173 Bdes

rifles and rocket-propelled grenades, but from March 1998 re-equipment by the West noticeably improved its performance in the field – although it could never match battle-hardened VJ and MUP units.

THE KOSOVO CONFLICT

The conflict can be divided into three phases: low-intensity warfare, 22 Apr 1996–28 Feb 1998; the Serb crackdown of Mar 1998–23 Mar 1999; and NATO intervention, 24 Mar–12 June 1999.

UÇK strategy was to ferment unrest which the Serbs would feel obliged to suppress with brutal force, thereby escalating the conflict and compelling the West to intervene, thus forcing the Serbs to grant Kosovan independence. Its covert agenda was to 'ethnically cleanse' Kosovo of Serbs and other minorities.

On 22 Apr 1996 UÇK guerrillas launched four simultaneous attacks on Serb police and civilians; they then began assaulting isolated Serbian police stations, setting up roadblocks in the countryside, attacking Serb and other minority civilians, and assassinating those Kosovo-Albanians considered to be collaborators. Montenegro remained neutral; but President Milosevic retaliated in Mar 1997 by massively reinforcing Serb forces in Kosovo. By Feb 1998 the 10,000-strong VJ Pristina Corps had tripled to 30,000 (30 per cent of total VJ strength), and the 6,500 Serbian Police, PJP and SAJ were tripled to about 19,500 with reservists and extra units. Meanwhile the UÇK employed classic guerrilla hit-and-run tactics while avoiding pitched battles.

In mid-Feb 1998 the UÇK advanced from its Drenica heartland and soon seized control of more than 30 per cent of Kosovo. This prompted Milosevic to order the 49,500 VJ and MUP to take the offensive on 28 Feb 1998, to retake UÇK-held areas and to eliminate the UÇK as a fighting force. This disguised his plan, Operation 'Horseshoe' *(Potkovica)*, to restore Serb control over Kosovo by killing the

Kosovo Liberation Army recruits parade before beginning training in northern Albania, 1999. They wear US Army summer camouflage uniforms, with the UÇK red, yellow and black Albanian eagle sleeve shield. Initial NATO enthusiasm for the UÇK turned to disillusion as this guerrilla army unscrupulously pursued a narrow nationalist agenda, carrying out 'ethnic cleansing' in their turn, and destabilizing regions beyond Kosovo's borders.

Kosovo-Albanians or driving them into exile in Albania and elsewhere, before repopulating the province with Serb refugees from Croatia and Bosnia. In Mar 1998, MUP forces spearheaded by PJP brigades attacked Drenica, held by III OZ, and later VJ units were deployed to seal off the Kosovo border with Albania and to provide artillery and helicopter-gunship support. The UÇK's move from guerrilla to conventional tactics proved premature, and by 28 July the Serbs had re-occupied Drenica and stood on the Albanian border. By Aug 1998 they had retaken 90 per cent of Kosovo, forcing the UÇK to abandon most of its territory; hundreds of fighters and civilians were killed, and about 360,000 civilians (36 per cent of the total Kosovar-Albanian population) were driven from their homes, many fleeing to Albania and Macedonia.

Milosevic's strategy to disguise ethnic cleansing as legitimate Serbian military action against a secessionist guerrilla force could not work indefinitely: the international community reacted, and on 23 Sept 1998 the UN demanded a ceasefire. They also demanded that Serb forces return to barracks, and revert to their peacetime strength of 6,500 Police and 10,600 VJ; and that by 27 Oct they permit access for an international monitoring force, under threat of NATO air-strikes. Milosevic pursued a deadly game of brinkmanship, convinced that he could still execute Operation 'Horseshoe' – either because a disunited international community would hang back, or because a few days or weeks of NATO air-strikes would provide a convenient smokescreen. Thus Milosevic initially complied with the UN demands, withdrawing forces into Serbia, and concentrating his remaining units around Malisevo in central Kosovo while the UÇK reclaimed lost territory. Meanwhile the Organization for Security and Co-operation in Europe (OSCE) established the Kosovo Verification Mission (KVM) on 25 Oct, deploying NATO aircraft and 2,000 OSCE personnel to Kosovo in November to verify compliance with the ceasefire.

During Nov 1998 Milosevic secretly returned some VJ and MUP units to Kosovo, and the next month fighting flared up. NATO's and the KVM's lack of reaction emboldened Milosevic, and on 15 Jan 1999

– following two UÇK ambushes and four police deaths in the vicinity – the 'Magla' unit, supported by Serbian Police and VJ T-55 tanks, attacked UÇK positions around the village of Racak near Stimplje (15 miles south of Pristina), killing 43 male civilians. Like Srebrenica, the atrocity galvanized international opinion; on 30 Jan NATO threatened air-strikes, and the six-nation Contact Group, formed in Jan 1997, called a peace conference at Rambouillet, France, for 6 Feb. The conference ended on 18 Mar without agreement; KVM monitors withdrew on 22 Mar, and on 24 Mar NATO launched its 79-day Operation 'Allied Force' air campaign.

NATO considered any target in Serbia, Vojvodina, Kosovo and neutral Montenegro legitimate, and 730 USAF and 325 other NATO aircraft flew 10,484 strike missions against VJ and MUP concentrations. Although the Serbs – particularly the armoured units – skilfully concealed their positions or offered dummy tanks as targets, the VJ suffered heavy punishment, losing 26 tanks, 153 other AFVs, 389 artillery pieces and about 5,000 dead. The Yugoslav AF was generally unsuccessful; its MiG-29 fighters briefly attacked targets in Kosovo and Bosnia, and AA missiles managed to shoot down a supposedly invulnerable US F-117 Nighthawk Stealth aircraft. Meanwhile bombers and cruise missiles from 13 US Navy and 21 other NATO aircraft carriers, assault ships, destroyers and frigates attacked military, government and 'dual use' installations with impunity, since the Yugoslav radar remained switched off to avoid retaliation. NATO ground forces were confined to the US Army's 2 Bn/505 Parachute Inf Rgt, 82 Abn Div at Tirana Airfield, Albania, ready for a ground invasion of Kosovo.

On 24 Mar 1999, as destruction mounted in Belgrade and Serbia, the MUP was subordinated to the VJ, forming an integrated command under 3 Army commander Gen Pavkovic. More than 50,000 VJ and MUP troops in Kosovo, supplemented by the JSO and Serb militias, launched Operation 'Horseshoe', rounding up Albanians in northern and central Kosovo and forcing them – by train, bus, car, cart or on foot – into NE

In January 2000 the ethnic-Albanian 'Presevo, Medvedja and Bujanovac Liberation Army' (UÇPMB) was formed as an off-shoot of the Kosovo Liberation Army, aiming to annex those three districts of southern Serbia. This UÇPMB machine-gunner is armed with an ex-VJ *Zastava* M80 7.62mm GPMG, a licence-built Soviet PK/PKS. He wears a black beret with a gilt UÇPMB badge, and a camouflage field uniform with that force's red, yellow and black sleeve shield.

Albania. 15 Armd Bde in Pristina and 211 Armd Bde from Serbia immediately secured the Pristina–Podujevo road, allowing 15 Armd, 37 & 125 Mot Bdes with MUP support to advance from Pristina into Drenica. 125 Mot Bde then advanced into southern Kosovo, joining 243 Mech Bde, which had just devastated Malisevo. By 29 Mar the outclassed UÇK were forced to retreat into Albania, leaving a few units in isolated enclaves. Now Serbian units – particularly 15 Armd and 125 Mot Bdes, SAJ, JSO, and about 2,000 Serb militiamen, joined in early April by 252 Armd, 549 Mot and 52 Mixed Arty Bdes – targeted civilians. They imprisoned many in makeshift detention camps, or killed the men and forced over 200,000 old people, women and children into Albania and Macedonia, sealing the borders to prevent refugees returning. By June 1999 about 15,000 Kosovar-Albanians were dead or missing, often buried in hidden graves.

On 27 May 1999 the ICTY indicted Milosevic for war crimes in Kosovo, and on 4 June Russia withdrew support from Serbia. The prolonged NATO campaign had caused immense damage to Serbia's infrastructure, and VJ recruits were failing to report for duty. Although MajGen Vladimir Lazarevic, commanding Pristina Corps, remained defiant, revitalized UÇK forces were advancing from NE Albania towards Pec and Prizren, pushing back VJ 125 Mot, 52 Mixed Arty and 63 Para Bdes, which were battered by NATO air-strikes. Milosevic admitted defeat on 4 June, and on the 10th signed a peace agreement with NATO; next day a ceasefire took force. On 12 June, under Operation 'Joint Guardian', NATO ground forces forming a 14-nation Kosovo Force (KFOR) under the British LtGen Michael Jackson advanced into Kosovo from Macedonia and Albania, as the 18,500-strong UÇK fanned across Kosovo to be greeted by the Kosovar-Albanians as liberators. Meanwhile, VJ and MUP forces retreated to Serbia – to the dismay of the Kosovar-Serb and some other minorities.

Agim Çeku, commanding the Kosovo Protection Corps, is photographed wearing its new uniform in September 1999. This unashamedly military uniform for a supposedly civilian organization comprises a royal-blue beret with a gilt badge, and a drab green shirt with the Croatian-style gold-on-black breast insignia of a *gjeneral lejtnant*. He wears a black-on-green name tag, and (unseen here) the TMK badge on the left upper sleeve, balanced by the GHQ badge on the right.

Southern Serbia

Under the peace agreement a 3-mile 'ground safety zone' was formed on the Serb side of the Kosovo-Serb border, open to lightly armed Serb Police but not to VJ or PJP. Nevertheless, the jubilant UÇK was determined to spread its insurgency to regions in southern Serbia and Macedonia containing ethnic Albanian minorities. On 26 Jan 2000 the Presevo, Medvedja and Bujanovac Liberation Army (*Ushtria Çlirimtare e Preshevës, Medvegjës dhe Bujanocit* – UÇPMB) was formed with UÇK commanders and ethnic Albanians, aiming to annex 'Eastern Kosova' – three districts in southern Serbia between Kosovo and Macedonia. The 1,500-strong force under Sefqet Musliu (HQ Dobrosin), divided into three Operational Zones – North, Centre and South – began attacking Serb Police in Presevo District; but on 24 May 2001 NATO, disenchanted with the uncompromising Albanian nationalism, allowed the VJ to send units, including elements of 63 Para and 72 Special Bdes, to re-occupy the ground safety zone, forcing a UÇPMB surrender on 26 May 2001.

Kosovo aftermath

On 10 June 1999 Kosovo, legally part of Serbia, was placed under the UN Interim Administration in Kosovo (UNMIK), with a governor ('administrator') committed to building peace, democracy, stability and self-government before returning Kosovo to Serbia. He was supported by KFOR (HQ Pristina), initially 48,000-strong, later 17,000, in five, later four sectors, each with a Multinational Brigade (MNB) or Multinational Task Force (MNTF), drawn from 36 national contingents: British, later Finnish, then Czech Sector (HQ Pristina) with MNB/MNTF Centre; French Sector (HQ Kosovska Mitrovica) with MNB/MNTF North, in Kosovo-Serb northern Kosovo; Italian Sector (HQ Pec), with MNB West, and German Sector (HQ Prizren), with MNB South – later combined to form MNB Southwest; and US Sector (HQ Gnjilane, later Urosavac), with MNB East, called Task Force Falcon. The 5,891-strong Russian contingent, deployed to the MNBs North, South & East to reassure the Kosovo-Serbs, returned home in May 2002.

On 26 Oct 1999 the UN formed the UNMIK Police with about 4,500 seconded policemen in national uniforms, and by 2004 about 7,000 of the Kosovo Police Service (KPS), divided among the five KFOR regions. The KPS had about 5,950 Kosovo-Albanian and 1,050 Kosovo-Serb personnel, wearing light blue uniforms with military ranks.

On 21 Sep 1999 the UÇK disbanded, and the Kosovo Protection Corps (*Trupat e Mbrojtjes së Kosovës* – TMK), formed ostensibly as an unarmed civil defence organization for natural disaster relief. The TMK, planned with 4,500 Kosovo-Albanians and 500 minority posts (no Serbs and almost no minorities joined), was divided into five regional response units, one for each KFOR Sector, and a mobile rapid response unit. The Kosovo-Albanian agenda under Çeku, the TMK commander, and Ibrahim Rugova – president on 4 Mar 2002, following free elections – was an independent Kosovo. On 21 Jan 2006 Rugova died of lung cancer, and on 10 Mar 2006 Çeku became prime minister, promising early Kosovo independence.

MACEDONIA

Macedonia in 1991 had 2,033,964 inhabitants: 64 per cent Macedonian-Slavs, 25 per cent Albanians, and 11 per cent of other minorities. The Macedonian-Slavs are Orthodox Christians, speaking a language close to Bulgarian and written in the Cyrillic alphabet.

On 8 September 1991 Macedonia, the most ethnically diverse state in the Balkans, won a uniquely peaceful 'velvet divorce' from Yugoslavia. Concerned that the Yugoslav Wars might claim her, Macedonia invited

UNPROFOR to establish Macedonia Command on 11 Dec 1992, stationing a 700-man Nordic Bn, and from 18 June 1993 two US Army companies, on her border with Albania and Kosovo. Later designated UN Preventative Deployment Force (UNPREDEP), this force was prematurely withdrawn on 28 Feb 1999.

From Mar 1999 about 360,000 Kosovo-Albanians crossed into NW Macedonia, almost doubling the local Albanian population, and triggering a refugee crisis; the UÇK manipulated this to encourage tensions between Macedonia's Slav and Albanian communities.

Macedonian Armed Forces

The *Armija na Republika Makedonija* (ARM) was established on 14 Feb 1992 from units of the Macedonian *Teritorijalna odbrana* (TO), primarily a Macedonian-Slav force with few ethnic Albanians. The JNA evacuated Macedonia on 27 Mar 1992, taking most of their heavy weapons, tanks and all aircraft. The UN arms embargo of Sept 1991 included Macedonia until 1996, leaving the ARM with light weapons only, and hampering its efforts to confront the Macedonian-Albanian insurgency. The ARM had 20,000 men with 100,000 reservists organized as follows: GHQ (Skopje): 1 Guards Bde, 8 Border Bde, Wolves *(Volci)* & Scorpions *(Skorpii)* Special Forces Units, an engineer and a signals rgt, MP & Military Academy Cadet battalions.

1 Corps (HQ Skopje-Kumanovo), 2 Corps (HQ Bitola) & 3 Corps (Stip) had a total of 19 bdes (1 armd, 2 mot, 6 inf, 9 light inf, 1 mixed arty), and two mixed arty rgts. The Air Force & AA Artillery (HQ Petrovec AFB, Skopje), formed June 1992, initially with no aircraft, eventually comprised: Air Bde – 301 Tspt Helicopter Sqn (1994); 201 AT Hcptr Sqn (Mar 2001); 101 Air Sqn (June 2001). AA Bde – SAM rgt, air warning rgt, and 10 AA bns; plus Falcons Para Detachment. The Lake Service had 5 patrol boats on Lake Ochrid.

Macedonian Interior Ministry forces

The ministry (MVR) controlled the Macedonian *Policija*, formed in Sept 1992 and comprising 7,000 full-time and reserve personnel deployed

At a Macedonian Army parade in 1996, *General-polkovnik* Dragoljub Bocinov – chief-of-staff from 3 March 1993 to 22 January 1996 – shakes hands with a recruit. Bocinov and other officers are wearing the M96 dark blue service uniform, while the recruit wears a greenish-brown service uniform with a red beret; he has slung his ex-JNA M70 assault rifle. The national title above the M95 flag badge is worn on the left sleeves of both uniforms by all ranks; and note the rank insignia of *polkovnik* on the shoulder board of the colonel on the right.

A Macedonian Army *vodnik I.klasa* in field uniform displays the woven M95 national flag – an eight-rayed yellow sun on a red ground – on the left side of the US PASGT helmet, and repeated below the bordered gold-on-black title 'MAKEDONIJA' on the left upper sleeve of his camouflage jacket. He is also wearing a camouflage armour vest, with his rank insignia attached – two curved bars over one straight bar, in white. Greek protests had led to the replacement in 1995 of the original 16-point star national emblem of 1992 with this sun motif. The Greeks resented the possible territorial implications of the star's resemblance to the 'star of Vergina' emblem of the historic Greek kingdom of Macedon.

across 123 districts. The Tigers *(Tigri)* Rapid Reaction Unit was trained for counter-insurgency missions and transport by Police Aviation Unit helicopters. The Lions *(Levi)* Special Police Unit, wearing red berets, was formed in 2001 specifically to fight the UÇK (NMET), and continued to hunt Macedonian-Albanian guerrillas until disbandment in Jan 2003.

National Liberation Army (Black Mountains and Tetovo)

In Jan 2000, Macedonian-Albanian nationalists formed this *Ushtria Çlirimtare Kombëtare në Malësinë e Tetovës* – UÇK (NMET). Effectively a branch of the Kosovo UÇK, it was commanded by Ali Ahmeti; from about 200 fighters it expanded to some 3,000 by Aug 2001, operating in the Black Mountains with its GHQ at Sipkovica village north of Tetovo. Six battalion-sized 'brigades' were led by ex-UÇK and UÇPMB fighters: 111, 113 'Imet Jashari' & 114 'Fadil Nimani Tigar', in the Black Mountains; 112 'Karadak' in Tetovo; 115 around Skopje, and 116 in Gostivar. Each contained several 'battalions' or companies, but 113 also had a 120-strong MP company and a 30-man *Mujahedin* platoon. There was also an independent unit of 150 *Mujahedin* from Afghanistan, Bosnia and Turkey under Selim Ferit. The UÇK (NMET) had some SAM

LEFT **Macedonian Army women privates wearing ex-JNA M59/85 helmets with M95 national flag transfers, and original Macedonian camouflage uniforms with the M95 flag on the left upper sleeve; the 'ARM' shield on the right sleeve is hidden at this angle (see commentary to Plate H1). They have ex-JNA light brown leather enlisted ranks' belts.**

RIGHT **Civilians across Bosnia-Herzegovina suffered terribly during the war, but none more than the rural Moslem population, whose religion and oriental dress earned them the permanent hatred of the Bosnian-Serbs and intermittent dislike from the Bosnian-Croats. Here a quietly heroic Bosnian policeman – wearing a Police shirt, jacket and trousers with civilian shoes, and armed with his service pistol, a *Zastava* M70 and hand grenades – leads Moslem civilians to what they must hope is safety. These victims of ethnic cleansing from near Tuzla – mostly old men, women and children – face an uncertain future.**

missiles and a captured T-55 tank. The Macedonian-Albanian minority further south along the Albanian border was less influenced by events in Kosovo, and did not join the insurgency. On 27 Sep 2001 the UÇK (NMET) officially disbanded, but many fighters joined the splinter Albanian National Army (*Armata Kombëtare Shqiptare* – AKSH), formed in 1999 and operating in Kosovo and Macedonia until Oct 2003.

THE YUGOSLAV WARS – AN OVERVIEW

The Yugoslav Wars lasted just over ten years, from 25 June 1991 to 13 August 2001. They were the culmination of bitterness harboured by the Slovenes, Croats, Bosnian-Moslems, Kosovo-Albanians and Macedonian-Slavs, all opposed to the leading political role claimed as of right by the Serbs since the foundation of Yugoslavia in 1918. This domination felt increasingly unbearable from 1990, as central and eastern Europe emerged from 50 years of Communism to take the first steps towards free market liberal democracy. Meanwhile, Slobodan

Milosevic used Serb pride and fear to further his political ambitions, offering to preserve Serb hegemony by force.

NATO states watched horrified as the wars in Slovenia, Croatia and Bosnia dragged Yugoslavia into a chaos that other ex-Communist states had avoided. The outside world was unwilling to infringe Yugoslav sovereignty by intervening, and slow to recognize Milosevic's ambitions; it was easy to avoid action by accusing all sides equally of irrational, bloodthirsty, 'tribal' nationalism. Slowly the USA and her allies recognized that Yugoslavia threatened European stability, and from August 1993 they intervened, finally achieving the Dayton Agreement, which ended the Croatian and Bosnian conflicts. This left the Kosovo issue; and when Milosevic sought a violent solution, NATO acted – but thus unintentionally encouraged Albanian nationalism, which threatened to destabilize Macedonia and even Serbia.

The Yugoslav Wars have transformed the western Balkans. Slovenia promptly took the path to prosperity and democracy, followed more slowly by Croatia and Macedonia, leaving the UN-controlled but still ethnicly divided Bosnia-Herzegovina struggling to catch up. Milosevic was deposed from power on 5 October 2001, sent to the Hague for trial by the ICTY on 5 February 2002, and died of natural causes in his cell on 11 March 2006. On 4 February 2003 the remaining state was renamed 'Serbia and Montenegro' instead of 'Yugoslavia', suggesting that Montenegro will achieve the independence for which she voted in May 2006, followed by Kosovo. Meanwhile Serbia, with a weak economy and an infrastructure still suffering from NATO bomb damage, is coming to terms with reduced political influence, and is painfully emerging from a decade as the pariah of Europe.

Many ordinary people across the ex-Yugoslav states look back sadly to the years before 1991, when so many ethnic groups seemed, at least superficially, to be able to co-exist in peace.

PLATE COMMENTARIES

A: BOSNIAN-MOSLEM FORCES, 1992
A1: Militiaman, Patriotic League; Sarajevo, April 1992
PL militiamen wore any available uniform items, including JNA olive-green and camouflage, TO blue, Bosnian Police blue and camouflage, US surplus camouflage, and civilian clothing. This militiaman wears a blue Civil Defence tunic with civilian jeans, a JNA belt and black boots. On the left upper sleeve a woven PL shield shows the coat-of-arms of Bosnian King Tvrtko and 'PL BiH'; the badge without the inscription is worn on his PL green beret.

A2: Officer, Territorial Defence Force; Tuzla, 1992
Before the war the Bosnian TO wore olive-grey or camouflage JNA uniforms or, to a limited extent, blue uniforms peculiar to Bosnia. From Apr 1992 a severe shortage of uniforms and equipment led to its personnel wearing anything available – here, an obsolete camouflage

JNA uniform, introduced in the 1970s for parachute, reconnaissance, border and special units. Initially some TO officers wore JNA rank insignia, but this was rare as it invited confusion with the enemy; this man's status is only identifiable by his JNA officers' belt and crossbelt. The woven TO shield on his left upper sleeve is the same as the PL patch apart from the inscription 'TO BiH'.

A3: *Samostalni inspektor*, Police Special Unit; Sarajevo, 1992

The Special Police wore three patterns of tiger-stripe camouflage plus the US Army woodland pattern. The pattern illustrated here resembles the US Army winter jacket and, unlike those worn in Croatia or Slovenia, has pointed pocket flaps. Senior officers of the Special Police wore a distinctive gold braid band on their camouflage field caps. The standard Yugoslav Police rank insignia

(introduced in Bosnia 5 May 1986) was worn, but with specific post-1992 rank titles for senior officers. The cap badge, initially the pre-1992 Yugoslav Police red enamel star on gold rays, was promptly replaced by a metal Bosnian coat-of-arms and later by a new Special Police badge. Regulations of 15 July 1993 prescribed that rank badges were to be worn on armbands on the right upper sleeve of camouflage uniforms, but usually they continued to be worn on shoulder straps.

B: BOSNIA-HERZEGOVINA ARMY, 1992–93
B1: *Vojnik*, winter 1992–93

The ABiH wore a wide variety of uniforms and civilian items. Towards the end of 1992, due to the lack of warm uniforms, they manufactured US Army pattern winter field uniforms from cloth found in a factory making women's

Rank insignia of Bosnia-Herzegovina Army, 31 Dec 1993–96; and of Moslem component, Federation of Bosnia-Herzegovina Army, 1996–31 May 1998

The first regulations of 1 Aug 92 were not implemented; the second were published 31 Dec 93. Officers wore insignia on dark blue shoulder straps (with edge piping, from 1 July 94), NCOs & privates on dark green straps. Rank was also worn on a rectangular left breast pocket patch on field uniform. On 1 June 98 these insignia were replaced by those of the Federation of Bosnia-Herzegovina Army.

Members of the Presidency of the Republic (1): Double 2.5mm gold braid edging; enamel Bosnian coat-of-arms (blue shield, gold edge & lilies, white bar) on gilt crossed swords; medium gold braid bar with 3 gilt metal lilies, thin gold braid bar.
Ministry of Defence officials (2): Same, but no thin bar.
General officers (3–5): Same, with 3–1 gilt lilies above coat-of-arms.
Field officers (6–8): Single 2.5mm gold edging, 3–1 gilt lilies above thin gold bar.
Captains & subaltern officers (9–12): 4–1 gilt lilies.
Senior NCOs (13–14): 2–1 silver metal lilies above thin silver braid bar.
Junior NCOs (15–18): 4–1 silver lilies.
Privates (19–20): 2–1 silver braid bars.
Vojnik (not illustrated): no insignia.

Key to ranks:
1 *Member of Presidency of the Republic*	9 Nadkapetan
	10 Kapetan
2 *Minister of Defence, Deputy Mnstr & senior officials*	11 Nadporucnik
	12 Porucnik
	13 Nadzastavnik
3 Armijski general	14 Zastavnik
4 Divizijski general	15 Nadcelnik
5 Brigadni general	16 Celnik
6 Brigadir	17 Nadvodnik
7 Pukovnik	18 Vodnik
8 Major	19 Desetar
	20 Razvodnik

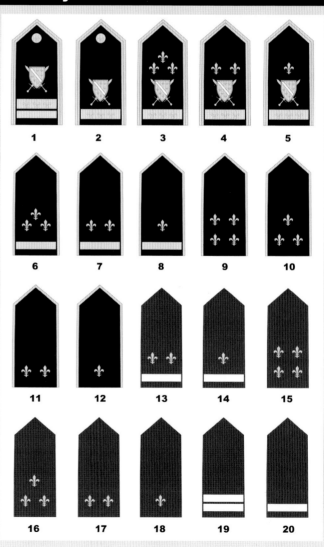

Dark blue cloth shoulder boards, slanted gold braid bars 8.4mm x 52mm, gilt metal lilies 15mm x 12mm. On camouflage field uniforms insignia were ordered worn on a right sleeve armband, but shoulder board insignia were usually preferred.

Interior Ministry officials (1–4): 6mm gold braid edging, 2 bars, 7–4 lilies.
Regional Police Chief (5): 2 bars & 3 lilies.
Police General (6): 2 crossed bars & 5 lilies.
Senior officers (7–9): 3 bars & 4–2 lilies.
Junior officers (10–12): 3mm gold braid edging, 3–1 bars & 1 lily.
NCOs (13–18): 5–1 bars & 2–1 lilies.

Key to ranks:
1 *Minister*
2 *Deputy Minister*
3 *Undersecretary*
4 *Asst Minister*
5 *Chief, Public Security Services Centre*
6 *General*
7 *Pukovnik*
8 *Podpukovnik*
9 *Major*
10 *Kapetan*
11 *Porucnik*
12 *Podporucnik*
13 *Nadzastavnik*
14 *Zastavnik*
15 *Glavni narednik*
16 *Nadnarednik*
17 *Narednik*
18 *Policajac*

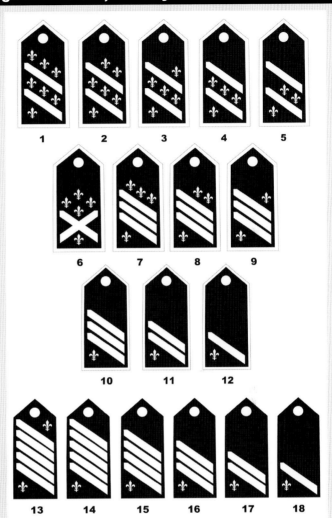

winter coats, retaining the original colours – including violet and pink. The ABiH badge, introduced Aug 1992, was worn on the left upper sleeve. Initially badges were worn bearing the name of the soldier's command; then gilt metal bars with lily flowers on the uppermost bar; and finally, at the end of 1993, conventional rank insignia as per regulations of 1 Aug 1992.

B2: Member of the Special Units, 1992

The ABiH Special Units, formed by the infamous Juka Prazina in July and Aug 1992, adopted several models of black uniforms or black civilian clothing or, where these were not available, camouflage uniforms, often worn with black headbands sometimes carrying the Bosnian cap shield, and with civilian trainers instead of military boots. The uniform illustrated seems to be modelled on one of the three Bosnian Police patterns. After Juka's Special Units were disbanded other ABiH special forces also adopted black; for example, the 'Black Swans' used a pattern resembling US Army summer and winter field uniforms.

B3: *Mujahed*, 1993

Mujahedin fighters wore a wide variety of camouflage uniforms and equipment, often brought from their native countries. This man wears a US Army surplus summer field uniform. Turbans and other Moslem headgear were very often worn instead of ABiH caps, and cap and tunic insignia often incorporated typically Moslem emblems, such as the star and crescent. A photo of Mujahedin of 7 Mtn Bde – the first explicitly Moslem unit in the ABiH – parading at Zenica in Oct 1992 shows white snow smocks worn over ABiH camouflage uniforms, and green headbands bearing white printed quotations from the Koran.

C: BOSNIAN-MOSLEM FORCES, 1994–95
C1: *Brigadni General*, Bosnia-Herzegovina Army; Sarajevo, 1994

In 1994 the ABiH finally introduced service uniforms, though only worn by generals and some field officers. They were brown, with gilt buttons embossed with a lily; a metal badge on the left breast pocket flap, with the inscription 'ARMIJA /REPUBLIKE/ BOSNE I HERCEGOVINE' replaced the sleeve badge worn on field uniforms. Rank insignia were published on 31 Dec 1993 and modified in July 1994. The badge on the peaked service cap was an enamelled ABiH cap shield on crossed swords in a wreath, all in gilt metal.

C2: *Nadkapetan*, 5 Corps, Bosnia-Herzegovina Army; Bihac, 1995

5 Corps personnel in NW Bosnia wore locally made uniforms with a unique camouflage pattern, and rank insignia on shoulder straps or as a modified patch version above the left breast pocket. Apart from the uniform worn by this senior captain, a wide variety of other camouflage or plain uniforms and civilian clothing were used. A variant of the standard ABiH arm shield was worn on the left upper sleeve, and some units wore badges on the right upper sleeve.

C3: *Vojnik*, National Defence of the Autonomous Province of Western Bosnia; Velika Kladusa, 1995

The breakaway NO wore the same wide variety of uniforms as ABiH 5 Corps, without rank insignia. After 21 Aug 1994 it was re-equipped by the Krajina Serbs with obsolete JNA uniforms including *Titovka* side caps with red star badges – the last troops in Yugoslavia to wear this badge. New arm badges were manufactured in the Republika Srpska, with the inscription 'NARODNA ODBRANA – ZAPADNA BOSNA'. The Western Bosnia Police, under Rasim Basic, wore Bosnian Police uniforms with a special badge on the left breast or left sleeve but no rank insignia.

D: BOSNIAN-SERB FORCES, 1992–95
D1: *General-major*, Republika Srpska Army, 1993

Soon after the outbreak of war the VRS introduced the traditional Serb M08 officers' peaked and enlisted ranks' peakless field cap in grey-green (here a variant in camouflage cloth); the badge was a copy of that introduced by the JNA after the red star was abolished in Oct 1991, but with the Serb national colours 'red-blue-white' replacing the Yugoslav 'blue-white-red'; general officers added a wreath. Generals also wore 3–1 thin and one medium gold braid rings and an ornamental gold braid chin cord. A circular

Rank insignia of Bosnia-Herzegovina Police, 3 June 1995–1996/7

Uniform-colour **shoulder boards**, with 6mm x 50mm gold braid bars and 30mm or 16mm gilt metal stars and wreaths. Stars showed a blue and white enamel Bosnia-Herzegovina coat-of-arms with gold lilies and edging, on gold rays. On camouflage uniforms insignia were worn on the **left breast**. Ranks corresponded with the officer's command; e.g. a 'chief of a 1st category police station' was a *Nadkapetan*, who received promotion only if he took a higher command – not merely for long service. In 1996/97 the Federal Police and individual cantons issued new regulations and introduced new insignia.

Interior Ministry officials (1–4): 30mm star in wreath above 3–0 bars.
Senior officers (5–7): 3–1 x 16mm stars above 2 bars.
Junior officers (8–11): 4–1 x 16mm stars above 1 bar.
NCOs (12–15): 4–1 stars; **(16)** 1 bar
Cadets (17): gold braid chevron.

Key to ranks:
 1 *Minister*
 2 *Deputy Minister*
 3 *Head of State Security Service*
 4 *Asst Mnstr; Ministry Secretary*
 5 Brigadir
 6 Pukovnik
 7 Major
 8 Nadkapetan
 9 Kapetan
10 Nadporucnik
11 Porucnik
12 Zastavnik
13 Glavni narednik
14 Nadnarednik
15 Narednik
16 Vodnik
17 *Police cadet*

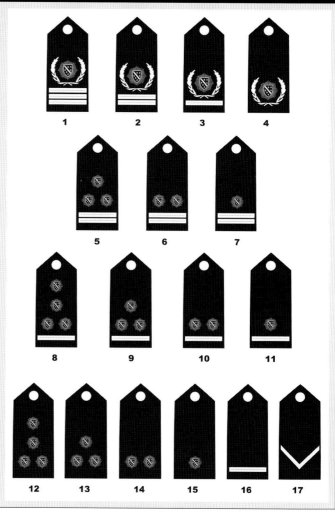

HVO command badges copied Croatian Army models, but with the Herceg Bosna coat-of-arms replacing the Croatian, and 'HVO' replacing 'RH'. Badges were of dark brown cloth, with gold or orange-yellow woven 'troplet' pattern or thin plain edging, stars, letters, crossed sword & branch, and red-&-white chequered ornate shield with gold ornamental crown and edging. Officials' badges (1–3) were ordered worn on the upper left sleeve, but in practice were worn on the left breast like (4–9).

Department of Defence officials (1–3): Oval badges, large coat-of-arms & sword-&-branch, and letters 'P', 'Z/P' or 'P/P', changed 28 Aug 1993 to 'M', 'Z/M' or 'P/M'. Later other, unofficial variations were introduced, e.g. 'N/VP' – Chief of Military Police.

Senior military commands (4–5): Round badges, 'HVO' in circle, small coat-of-arms & sword-&-branch, 1–0 stars.

Junior military commands (6–9): Round badges, 'HVO' in circle, 4–0 stars.

Key to commands:

1 *Head of Dept of Defence (28.8.93>, Mnstr of Defence)*
2 *Deputy Head (Deputy Mnstr)*
3 *Asst Head (Asst Mnstr)*
4 *Corps/ Operational Zone/ Corps Region Commander*
5 *Brigade Commander*
6 *Battalion Commander*
7 *Company Commander*
8 *Platoon Leader*
9 *Section Leader*

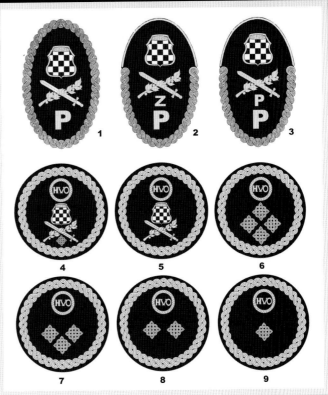

embroidered badge showing the Serb national colours, with the Cyrillic inscription 'VOJSKA REPUBLIKE SRPSKE' on the outer border, was worn on the left upper sleeve. Some units wore unit badges on the right upper sleeve. The VRS wore JNA rank insignia on the left breast of the field tunic and shirt. In 1996 they introduced service and dress uniforms with a new pattern of shoulder-strap rank insignia. This major-general wears a thick winter jacket not normally available to lower ranks.

D2: *Vodnik I. klase, Republika Srpska* Army Commandos, 1994

The VRS was equipped by the JNA/VJ and therefore wore all models of Yugoslav tiger-stripe or leaf camouflage uniforms, as well as their own models. The leaf-pattern overall worn by this NCO was originally introduced for VJ paratroopers, although the VRS preferred the tiger-stripe variant. Note the small infantry branch badge above his rank insignia, all in gilt metal.

D3: *Major*, Bosnian-Serb Special Police Detachment, 1995

The Bosnian-Serb Police participated in combat operations, usually wearing Serbian Police blue-grey camouflage uniforms. This officer is wearing the same model uniform as the VRS soldier in D2 but in Police pattern. Initially the M92 Serbian Police cap badge was worn, comprising a rectangular enamel red-blue-white Serbian flag on a gilt metal ornamental backing, but in 1995 it was replaced with a more explicitly Serbian woven badge, showing a gold crowned two-headed eagle in a gold wreath on a red oval backing. A

white-framed Cyrillic title 'MILICIJA', worn on a dark blue arc on both upper sleeves, was replaced in 1995 with a woven Serbian red-blue-white shield on a crowned two-headed eagle with 'POLICIJA' above. The standard pre-1992 shoulder strap rank insignia, as worn in all the ex-Yugoslav republics, were retained; they were replaced from 1995 to Oct 1999 with gold braid insignia on the shoulder straps and military rank titles. NCOs wore broad and medium chevrons point up; subaltern officers, 1–4 crosses; field officers, 1–3 crosses above a chevron point down.

E: BOSNIAN-CROAT FORCES, 1992–95
E1: *Brigadir*, 1 Guards Brigade, Croatian Defence Council, 1994

The HVO wore US Army surplus uniforms or Croatian-made copies and variants; this officer of the élite unit wears a hooded winter field jacket. The standard HVO woven badge on the left upper sleeve comprises a wreathed Croatian chequered shield above crossed rifles and 'HVO'; on the right upper sleeve is the woven brigade badge. Above the right breast pocket a brown cloth strip bears the gold inscription 'HRVATSKO VIJECE OBRANE'; other versions, which included the unit name, were also worn but eventually abolished. All the Guards brigades wore berets, each with metal brigade badges: 1, black (chequers on gold disc); 2, grey (dragon, knight's arm and sword); 3, black (hawks on black triangle); and 4, dark red (chequers and silver '4'). The HVO wore HV rank insignia, but retained the NCO rank of *Stozerni vodnik* (abolished in the HV

Herceg Bosna introduced Croatian Police rank insignia but with different titles for Department of Internal Affairs (OUP) officials. Dark blue shoulder straps bore metal six-point stars and braid bars and chevrons, with or without edging. On 18 Mar 93 these insignia was modified; and on 28 Aug 93, when Herceg Bosna became a Republic, the OUP was redesignated a Ministry (MUP) and officials received new titles. New insignia were introduced in 1997–98 in different Federation cantons.

OUP/ MUP officials (1–4): 4–1 gold stars, over 1x 10mm & 2x 20mm gold bars; gold edging.

Senior officers (5–8): 4–1 gold stars, over 2x 20mm goldbars; gold edging.

Junior officers (9, 11–12): 3–1 gold stars, over 1x 20mm gold bar; blue edging.

Probationary officers (10 & 13): 3 or 1 gold stars over 1x 20mm white bar; white edging.

Senior constables (14–16): 1–0 gold stars over 2–1 gold chevrons over 1x 10mm gold bar; blue edging.

Junior constables (17–19): 3–1x 10mm gold bars; blue edging.

Probationary Junior Constable & Police Cadet (20 & 21): 2–1 white bars, no edging.

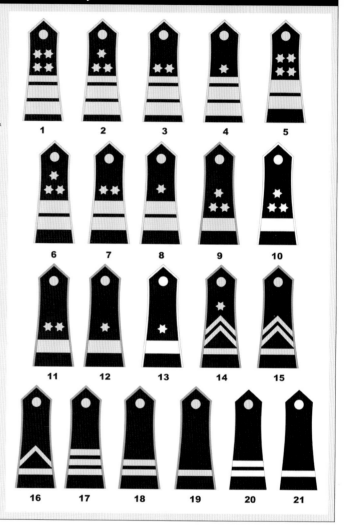

Key to ranks:

1 Head of OUP (28.8.93>, Mnstr of Internal Affairs)
2 Deputy Head (Deputy Mnstr)
3 Asst Head (18 Mar 1993>, Chief of Public Security)
4 Asst Head (18 Mar 1993>; 28 Aug 1993>, Asst Mnstr)
5 Glavni inspektor
6 Visi inspektor 1.klase
7 Visi inspektor
8 Samostalni inspektor
9 Inspektor 1.klase
10 Pripravnik za inspektora 1.klase (probationary, 18.3.93>)
11 Inspektor
12 Mladji inspektor
13 Pripravnik za mladjeg inspektora (probationary)
14 Visi policajac
15 Stariji policajac 1.klase
16 Stariji policajac
17 Policajac 1.klase
18 Policajac
19 Mladji policajac
20 Pripravnik za mladjeg Policajca (probationary)
21 Police Cadet

on 20 June 1995), until the adoption of Bosnia-Herzegovina Federation Army insignia in 1998.

E2: *Stozerni vodnik*, Military Police, Croatian Defence Council, 1995

The HVO beret badge showed a curved enamel red-and-white chequered shield with a gilt metal 'troplet' ornamental top. The MPs followed HV practice by adopting in 1992 the gilt HV MP badge worn on a square leather fob from the left breast pocket. Due to irregularities and misuse of these badges, new badges were introduced in 1994; these showed a stylized gilt falcon with the HVO chequers and the inscription 'VOJNA POLICIJA' (Military Police).

E3: *Porucnik*, Croatian Defence Forces Militia, 1992

The HOS used any available camouflage uniforms, usually surplus US Army or Croatian copies, but also favoured black uniforms modelled on the camouflage clothing. The standard HOS woven badge, as worn in Croatia, appeared on the left upper sleeve, but others were also worn, including the blue enamel ABiH shield as worn on this lieutenant's beret beside the chequered shield. The HOS wore HVO field uniform rank insignia on the left breast.

F: ETHNIC ALBANIAN FORCES, 1999–2001
F1: Officer, Kosovo Liberation Army, 1999

Ethnic Albanian guerrillas in Kosovo, southern Serbia and Macedonia used any camouflage uniforms they could find, capture or smuggle, often combined with civilian – particularly black – items; this officer wears a German Army M94 camouflage uniform. On the left upper sleeve the UÇK wore a red cloth straight-sided shield with a black two-headed Albanian eagle, gold piping, the inscription 'USHTRIA ÇLIRIMTARE E KOSOVËS' and the initials 'UÇK'. A smaller round cloth badge was worn on a black or red beret or peaked camouflage field cap. No rank insignia were worn.

F2: Volunteer of Presevo, Medvedja & Bujanovac Liberation Army, 1999

The UÇPMB wore the same sleeve and beret badges as the Kosovo UÇK, but with the inscription 'USHTRIA ÇLIRIMTARE E PRESHEVËS, MEDVEGJËS DHE BUJANOCIT' and the initials 'UÇPMB'. This fighter is wearing an obsolete 1960s JNA camouflage uniform, and has pulled on a woollen face mask to avoid recognition by the Serbian Police.

F3: Military Policeman, National Liberation Army (Black Mountains and Tetovo); Macedonia, 2001

The UÇK (NMET) wore the same uniforms as the Kosovo UÇK, with similar red cloth sleeve and beret badges showing a black two-headed eagle, the black inscription 'USHTRIA ÇLIRIMTARE KOMBËTARE' and the initials 'UÇK'. This man wears black civilian clothing, and on the left upper sleeve a white-edged black brassard with a beret badge and the white initials 'PU' for Policia Ushtarake –

Military Police; there was also a plain black armband with larger white letters. The Albanian National Army probably wore similar beret and sleeve badges, with the inscription 'ARMATA KOMBËTARE SHQIPTARE' and the initials 'AKSH'.

G: YUGOSLAV & SERBIAN FORCES IN KOSOVO, 1999
G1: Porucnik, Yugoslav Army

This VJ officer wears M91 camouflage winter field uniform in the common leaf pattern. The standard M92 embroidered VJ badge was worn on the left upper sleeve, but only élite units wore unit badges on the right sleeve. JNA rank insignia and titles were retained, with gilt metal or cloth badges worn above the left breast pocket – or, on summer uniform, on the pocket flap or pocket itself. The M92 Army enlisted ranks' cap badge depicted a two-headed eagle on a small gold oak wreath and a blue-white–red flag on crossed silver swords; officers had a larger wreath, general officers even larger. The

Rank insignia of Republic of Serbia Police, 5 April 1996–July 2002

Serbian police introduced military rank titles and new general officers' insignia in Apr 96. Uniform-colour **shoulder straps** displayed insignia, including five-point stars, on all types of uniform except the winter blue-grey camouflage uniform, where they were worn on the **left breast**. Later, black subdued rank insignia were introduced for combat uniforms.

General officers (1–3): 3-1 gold braid stars & branches; gold embroidered leaf edging.

Field officers (4–6): 3-1 gilt metal stars, over 2x 16mm gold braid bars; gold edging.

Captains & subaltern officers (7–9): 3-1 gilt metal stars over 1x 16mm gold braid bar; gold edging.

Probationary subaltern officer – university graduate (10): 1 silver metal star over 1x 16mm white braid bar; blue edging.

Warrant officers (11–13): 3-1 gilt metal stars over 1x 10mm gold braid bar; blue edging.

Probationary warrant officer – 2-year college diploma (14): 1 silver metal star over 1x 10mm silver braid bar; blue edging.

Senior NCOs (15–17): 3-1 gold braid chevrons over 1x 10mm gold braid bar; blue edging.

Junior NCOs (18–20): 3-1 gold braid chevrons; blue edging.

Probationary NCO – secondary diploma (21): 1 white braid chevron; blue edging.

Police College Cadets (22–25): 3-0 white braid chevrons over 1x 16mm white braid bar; blue edging.

Police Secondary School Cadets (26–29): Roman numerals IV-I over 1x 16mm white braid bar; blue edging.

Key to ranks:

1	General-pukovnik	
2	General-potpukovnik	
3	General-major	
4	Pukovnik	
5	Potpukovnik	
6	Major	12 Zastavnik
7	Kapetan	13 Mladji zastavnik
8	Porucnik	14 *Probationary warrant officer*
9	Potporucnik	15 Stariji vodnik I.klase
10	*Probationary subaltern officer*	16 Stariji vodnik
11	Stariji zastavnik	17 Vodnik I.klase

18 Vodnik
19 Mladji vodnik I.klase
20 Mladji vodnik
21 *Probationary NCO*
22–25. *4th–1st year Police College Cadets*
26–29. *4th–1st year Police Secondary School Cadets*

beret colours were: maroon – Guards Bde; maroon (outstretched eagle beret & right sleeve badge) – 63 Para Bde; black (outstretched eagle beret badge, falcon right sleeve badge) – 72 Special Bde; black (eagle right sleeve badge) – MPs; greenish-brown – other Army branches; dark blue (Navy beret badge) – Navy; grey-blue (AF beret badge) – Air Force.

G2: *Vodnik*, Serbian Special Police

Almost all Serbian Police switched to blue-grey tiger-stripe pattern camouflage uniforms in Oct 1991. A yellow-framed Cyrillic title 'MILICIJA' on a dark blue arc was worn on both upper sleeves – from 1995, above a baroque woven shield edged light blue with the Serbian red–blue–white tricolour; in Jan 1997 the title changed to 'POLICIJA'. This NCO wears the woven M95 PJM (from Jan 1997, PJP) badge on the right upper sleeve. The badge on the blue beret was the M92 rectangular enamel Serbian flag on a gilt metal ornamental backing. Later, peaked blue caps or camouflage field caps were introduced; from 1 Jan 1996 officers wore a curved woven shield edged gold with the Serbian red–blue–white tricolour in a gold wreath (NCOs and other ranks, white edging and wreath), on a dark blue

cloth backing. At first the standard pre-1992 shoulder strap rank insignia were retained, with standard Police rank titles, but in Jan 1996 military-style rank titles were introduced.

G3: Policeman, Serbian Special Operations Unit

The élite JSO was well equipped with several camouflage uniforms suitable for any type of combat; this officer wears the winter model. When not in combat JSO troops wore a red beret with a gold, silver and black shield badge (earning them the nickname 'Red Berets'), and a blue neck scarf. A ceremonial uniform comprised the red beret, a white shirt, red waistcoat, dark blue tunic and trousers.

H: MACEDONIAN FORCES, 2001

H1: *General-major*, Macedonian Army

In 1993 the ARM introduced a greenish-brown service uniform, changing to dark blue-grey in 1996. Berets were introduced in 1993 as the only headgear: Army – brown; Air Force – blue; service uniform – red. In 1996 peaked service caps were introduced, with a gold braid chin strap and two rows of gold leaves on the peak for general

Rank insignia of Macedonian Army, 1992 to date

Insignia from end 1992 to 1996 were as combat uniform **breast patches**; after 1996 **shoulder strap** insignia were introduced for dress, service and everyday uniform. On 21 Feb 2000, generals' ranks were modified to conform with NATO '1–4 star' rank structure, and their insignia slightly modified.

General officers (1–4): 4–1 gold eight-point stars over gold tobacco-leaf wreath, gold braid edging. **Breast badge:** 4–1 8mm gold braid bars under gold wreath.

Field officers (5–7): 3–1 gold stars over 15mm gold braid bar. **Breast badge:** 3–1x 4mm curved gold bars over 1x 14mm & 1x 6mm straight bars.

Subaltern officers (8–11): 4–1 gold stars. **Breast badge:** 4–1x 4mm gold curved bars over 1x 14mm straight bar.

Senior NCOs (12–13): 2–1 silver stars over white 15mm braid bar. **Breast badge:** 2–1x 4mm white curved bars over 1x 14mm & 1x 6mm white straight bars.

Junior NCOs (14–17): 4–1 stars. **Breast badge:** 4–1x 4mm white curved bars over 1x 14mm white straight bar.

Privates (18–20) – breast badge only: 3–1x 7mm red curved bars.

Vojnik (not illustrated): no insignia.

Key to ranks:	
1 General na armija (21.2.00>, General)	11 Potporucnik
2 General-polkovnik (General-potpolkovnik)	12 Znamenosec I.klasa (1996> Zastavnik I.klasa)
3 General-potpolkovnik (General-major)	13 Znamenosec (1996> Zastavnik)
4 General-major (Brigaden general)	14 Postar vodnik I.klasa
5 Polkovnik	15 Postar vodnik
6 Potpolkovnik	16 Vodnik I.klasa
7 Major	17 Vodnik
8 Kapetan I.klasa	18 Pomlad vodnik
9 Kapetan	19 Desetar
10 Porucnik	20 Razvodnik

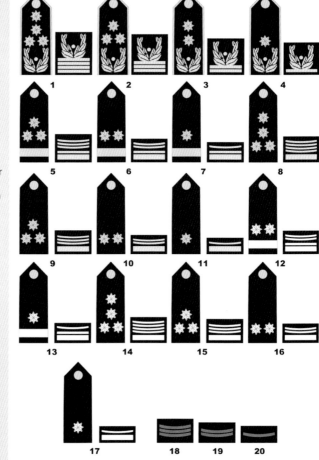

Macedonian police introduced military rank titles on 2 August 1994, with four-point metal stars and braid edgings on dark blue shoulder straps & loops. On 3 Jan 2002 four general officers' ranks were introduced, with 4-1 gold stars on the general's shoulder strap (1).

General (1): 1 gold star on red loop with gold braid edging (not illustrated). From 4 Oct 1997, gold star & gold braid tobacco-leaves, over gold braid 'troplet' bar, on dark blue shoulder strap piped gold.
Senior officers (2–4): 3-1 gold stars on loop between double 5mm gold edgings.
Junior officers (5, 6 & 8): 3-1 gold stars on loop between single 5mm gold edgings.
Probationary lieutenant & second lieutenant (7 & 9): 2 & 1 gold stars on loop between 5mm silver braid edgings.
Senior NCOs (10–11): 2-1 silver stars on loop between double 5mm silver braid edgings.
Junior NCO (12–13): 2-1 silver stars on loop between single 5mm silver braid edgings.
Probationary corporal (14): Silver star on loop between single 5mm silver braid edgings

Key to ranks:
1 General
2 Polkovnik
3 Potpolkovnik
4 Major
5 Kapetan
6 Porucnik
7 Pripravnik za porucnik
8 Potporucnik
9 Pripravnik za potproucnik
10 Vis vodnik 1. klasa
11 Vis vodnik
12 Postar vodnik
12 Vodnik
14 Pripravnik za vodnik

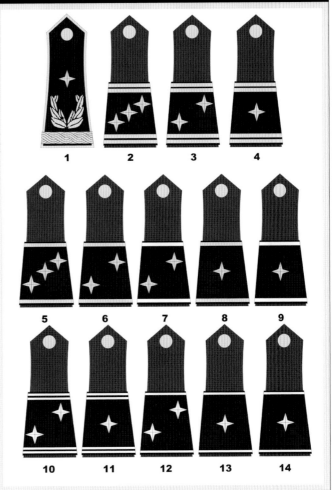

officers, a black leather chinstrap for other officers, and one row of leaves on the peak for field ranks. The M93 service uniform rank insignia consisted of straight and curved bars, with a wreath for general officers; in 1996 new service uniform rank insignia were introduced on the shoulder straps, while the M93 insignia were retained as breast ranking on field uniforms. The Macedonian flag – from Feb 1992 a yellow 16-point star, replaced in Oct 1995 by a yellow eight-rayed sun, on a red rectangle – was worn on the left upper sleeve, below a black arc edged gold with a gold Cyrillic title 'MAKEDONIJA'. The ARM badge worn on the right upper sleeve was a black cloth shield edged gold below the initials 'ARM', with crossed rifles in a wreath, all woven in gold.

H2: *Vodnik I. klasa*, Macedonian Army
In 1993 the ARM introduced the camouflage field uniforms illustrated (though others were occasionally worn, most often US Army surplus), with field rank insignia on the left breast.

The JNA M59 helmet was worn, and later the distinctive M93 Eurokompozit PPS model, painted brownish-green; the M92 or M95 Macedonian flag was displayed on the left side, and an M93 gilt metal sun with a black boss and the initials 'ARM' on the front.

H3: Constable, Macedonian Police
The Macedonian Police wore uniforms in the same camouflage pattern as other ex-Yugoslav republics, but of a distinctive model lacking the left upper sleeve pocket. A black shield was worn on the left upper sleeve, showing a gold woven Cyrillic title 'REPUBLIKA MAKEDONIJA' and 'POLICIJA', 'POLICE' in English, and Cyrillic initials 'PM' in a wreath. On the right upper sleeve was a black rectangle with the gold woven Cyrillic title 'POLICIJA'. Special Police wore the same uniforms with unit arm badges. New rank insignia were introduced in Oct 1994 – featuring varying numbers of four-point stars and transverse bands (see above) – but were rarely worn on camouflage field uniforms.

INDEX